E-PUBLISHING AND WEB TECHNOLOGY

E-PUBLISHING AND WEB TECHNOLOGY

P Balasubramanian
MBA,MCA,MA,MLISc,M Phil,PhD
University Librarian
Manonmaniam Sundaranar University
Tirunelveli-627012
Tamil Nadu –India.

S.Meena
Msc, MBA, NET, PhD
Librarian
Pachaiyappa's College
Chennai - 600030

Ess Ess Publications
New Delhi

E-PUBLISHING AND WEB TECHNOLOGY

ISBN : 978-81-947398-8-3

Price : Rs. 800/-

First Published 2021

Published by:
Ess Ess Publications
4831/24, Ansari Road,
Darya Ganj,
New Delhi-110 002.
INDIA
Phones: 23260807, 41563444
Fax: 41563334
E-mail: info@essessreference.com
www.essessreference.com

Cover Design by *Patch Creative Unit*

Printed and bound in India

Contents

Preface

Electronic publishing also referred to as E-Publishing includes the digital publication of e-books, EPUBs, and electronic articles and the distribution of written information digitally through CD-ROMs, DVDs, portable document files(PDF) or online over the internet or other networks. True digital publishing takes advantage of networking tools and multimedia tools and capabilities. The web is a truly revolutionary advance in ability to disseminate information. However, web publishing has disadvantages, some temporary, some inherent. For example ability to search is one of the core advantages of a digital format which makes it easier to find whatever you need weeding out the duplicate results and thus saving you some valuable time and needless efforts. Electronic publishing has also removed much of the cost and risk involved in print publishing. With web publishing, more information can be stored electronically than on paper and e-published material can be sent across the globe in a few seconds. The actual time it takes for a book to get e-published is much faster than print format. Where going the old fashioned way might take, in worst case scenario, up to two years, e-publishing can be as quick as two to three weeks to only a few months after acceptance. Where paper publishers usually try to obtain as many rights a possible , the e-publisher usually retains none. That means the author gets to keep the rights to his/her work and even has the option to take it to a paper publisher at a later date. On the other hand, once printed, the details of a paper journal remain constant, thus finding them again is pretty simple, and however web sites change their URLs or frequently disappear altogether thus making the virtual book inaccessible.

P. Balasubramanian

S. Meena

Acknowledgements

The authors feels extremely indebted to Dr. K. Pitchumani, Hon'ble Vice-Chancellor, Manonmaniam Sundaranar University, Tirunelveli – 627 012. We also thank all the teaching and non-teaching staff members of the Manonmaniam Sundaranar University, for giving us constant encouragement for writing this book.

We would be failing in our duty if we do not acknowledge the services of Ess Ess Publications, New Delhi for their efforts in bringing out this book in a record time. Suggestions for further improvement of the book are most welcome.

P. Balasubramanian

S. Meena

Unit 1

OBJECTIVES

- To learn the international standard codes such as ASCII
- To understand the Indian languages representation in computers
- To know the techniques and standards for handling Indian languages in computers

1.1. INTRODUCTION

Content is a reusable collection of metadata (columns), workflow, behavior, and other settings for a category of items or documents in a Microsoft Share Point Foundation 2010 list or document library. Content types enable you to manage the settings for a category of information in a centralized, reusable way.

For example, imagine a business situation in which you have three different types of documents: expense reports, purchase orders, and invoices. All three types of documents have some characteristics in common; for one thing, they are all financial documents and contain data with values in currency. Yet each type of document has its own data requirements, its own document template, and its own workflow. One solution to this business problem is to create four content types. The first content type, Financial Document, could encapsulate data requirements that are common to all financial documents in the organization. The remaining three, Expense Report, Purchase Order, and Invoice, could inherit common elements from Financial Document. In addition, they could define characteristics that are unique to each type, such as a particular set of metadata, a document template to be used in creating a new item, and a specific workflow for processing an item.

You can use each of the content types in this example on any document library in the site hierarchy, and you can use all of them together on the same document library. When business requirements change, you can modify the content types to meet the new requirements and push down the updates to any document library where the content type is used.

1.2. CONTENT TYPES ENCAPSULATE DATA REQUIREMENTS

Content types are a means of encapsulating the data requirements for a category of information. A content type can include the following information:

- The metadata, or properties, you want to assign to this type. These are represented by site columns added to the list or document library when you add the content type. For more information, see Columns.
- Custom New, Edit, and Display forms to use with this content type. For more information, see Custom Information in Content Types.
- Workflows available for items of this content type. These can be defined to start automatically based on a selected event or condition, or through user selection. For more information, see the Work flow Associations property.
- For document content types, the document template on which to base documents of this type. For more information, see Document Template Element (Content Type).
- Any information necessary for custom solutions that are associated with this content type. You can store this information in the content type as one or more XML documents. For more information, see Custom Information in Content Types.

1.2.1. Content Types Enable Content Standardization

Because content types can be defined independently of any specific list or document library, you can make a given content type available for the lists on multiple SharePoint Foundation sites. This enables you to centrally define and manage the types of content you store in your site collection. For example, you could define a Legal Document content type to ensure that all legal documents track the same metadata, even if those documents are created and stored in multiple sites.

1.2.2. Content Types Are File Format Independent

Content types are independent of file formats. For

example, suppose you create a content type to represent a business plan. This content type could be applied to any file format. You might have the following:

- Microsoft Word documents that contain background information
- Microsoft Excel workbooks that contain a financial plan
- Microsoft PowerPoint presentations for the venture capital pitch
- Windows Media files of demos
- SharePoint Foundation list items that contain the specified metadata

You can assign the Business Plan content type to all of these files. You can also assign content types to items that do not have a file at all, such as list items or folders.

1.2.3. Content Type Creation

You can create column and content types in three ways:

- Using the SharePoint Foundation user interface.
- Using the SharePoint Foundation object model.
- Deploying a Feature that installs the content type based on an XML definition file. For more information, see Using Features in SharePoint Foundation.

1.3. DIGITALCONTENT

Digital Content generally refers to the electronic delivery of fiction which is shorter than book-length, nonfiction, documents and other written works of shorter length. Publishers of digital content deliver shorter sized works to the consumer via download to handheld and other wireless devices. Technology used for delivering digital content includes Adobe PDF, XML, HDML, WAP (Wireless Application Protocol) and other technologies. The security of the data being delivered is the major concern of publishers who want to ensure they can deliver digital content without the risk of someone copying the work and selling or giving away the works. The market for wireless content, which is being developed to deliver content to everything from phones, handhelds, microwaves and even clothes, is a potentially enormous market. This fact has the major media companies and publishers scrambling not to be left out of the digital content arena.

1.3.1. Managing Digital Content

Contents in a digital library are organized and managed for the purpose of immediate access to the target audience. How contents are developed and managed, is a critical issue to the longterm success of digital library services, especially when technical resources are limited. Content management includes the following key functions:

- Selection and acquisition
- Indexing
- Storage
- Retrieval
- Maintenance and
- Rights management.

1.3.2. Selection and Acquisition

Libraries select content according to a well-defined collection development policy. Such policy manifests the mission of a library and determines how budgets on materials expended. There are two key challenges in content selection i.e. cost and quality. Firstly, librarian should consider the cost of acquisition. Intellectual property rights are important considerations, but the cost of digitization and maintenance must also be taken into account. Secondly, librarian should consider the quality of the content before acquiring it. This is more problematic consideration because issue of authorities as well as veracity arises. As soon as decision about selection is made, content must be acquired. For objects, which are already in digital form, the file transfer through networks or mass storage is straightforward and as long as file formats are well specified. In case of traditional objects, digitization must be done. Scanners for text and images range in quality on several dimensions (i.e. output resolution, value and conditions of physical objects and speed) are required. In addition to these technical challenges policy decision must be made. For example, which resolution and formats to adopt, which text to OCR subsequently error correct, how to link different representation for multiple media from single collections.

1.3.3. Indexing

Once content has been selected and acquired, it will be added to the collection in such a way that users may retrieve it easily. And thus, indexing is required for digital content to search and access in a selective way like OPAC for printed content. Decisions are to be taken regarding what to be indexed (author, keywords, phrase, etc), how the content and index files are linked, what sort of access points are provided, etc. Indexing strategy comprises not only of what types of fields are to be indexed, but how they are to be treated (exhaustive or sparse). Automatic indexing techniques are used to index the content of digital library. Texts are indexed using vector-space or probabilistic information retrieval models that provide access through weighted values for all but a few cornmon words, and thus the classification system itself is empirically determined from the data as a by-product of the indexing. Inquiry system is the most successful example of this approach used as the retrieval engine in many digital library projects (e.g., Library of congress). These approaches based on traditional approach of manually assigning object to a limited number of manually constructed concept classes (classification system) represented in a control vocabulary (e.g., Library of Congress subject headings or medical subject headings). Other automatic techniques index object to mathematically abstract concept classes. Several www-based services use a hybrid approach by manually creating classification system and then using automatic techniques to assign objects. Most retrieval systems for images, video, audio recordings and other non-textual objects have depended on text items such as title, creator name or manually assigned subject headings for retrieval. It seams certain that digital library research and development activity of 1990s will ensure that considerable progress is made in automatic indexing for textual and non textual objects. New indexing challenges will emerge as more dynamic objects (e.g., virtual conference proceeding, active networks) are added to digital libraries. The temporal nature of such objects will require ongoing indexing techniques.

1.3.4. Storage

The next thing is how to store the content of digital library. Decisions regarding procuring suitable hardware, software, networking, etc. are to be made at this stage. Storage is mainly a technical requirement, although new media may complicate storage decision and costing. When data are to deliver continuously (e.g., streaming video or audio) rather than as discrete files, alternative technologies are required. Drives and database management software that operate continuously have different engineering requirements from drives optimized for bursts of data. Large digital repositories are required multiple level of mass storage media (e.g., disk, tape, etc.) and mechanical robots to locate and mounts the media. Various supercomputer centers are using tape robots that store and access to many terabytes of data. Digital libraries will surely apply such technology just as libraries of today apply movable shelving and complex conveyer systems to move physical materials.

1.3.5. Retrieval

Retrieval is another major issue, as far as digital library

content and its access is concerned. Ultimately, users must be able to retrieve the content, which have been selected, indexed and stored by the librarians. During 1970s to 1980s, a large number of libraries invested heavily in computerizing cataloging and circulation functions to give users better access and services. Online Public Access Catalogues (OPACs) have long provided author, title, and limited subject access to local holdings (and more recently to union holdings across to multiple libraries). The expectation for digital collection is that catalogue should seamlessly link to the digital content itself so that remotely located users can find and display not only bibliographic records, but also primary information objects. In physical libraries, the card catalogues or OPAC is physically distinct from the items on shelves. These distinctions are difficult to make in electronic environments because everything is displayed on the same physical screen and thus, the boundaries between metadata and primary data are often blurred. Distinguishing metadata and primary data is not a trivial problem in rich collections. In homogenous collections it is possible to define a unit of primary content (e.g., a book rather than a character or series), but this is more problematic in heterogeneous collections containing findings aids, manuscripts, bitmaps, videos and hypertexts. Expectation to provide primary data with metadata yields several challenges to librarians. The challenges are first to extract and provide multiple levels of representation and second to provide user with control mechanisms to move from high-level surrogates to detailed objects. Huge challenges remain in creating surrogates for digital content. Today most retrieval is facilitated through words, titles, captions, manually created subscriptions, automatically extracted keywords and so on. There is enormous attention focused on creating non textual surrogates such as colour and shape characterizations for images and speaker identification schemes for audio recordings, but there are more difficult metadata issues looming as more contents are not stored at all but created on the fly according to the specifications of the users. Today digital libraries offer access to primary content using a variety of access tools. An active area of research is user interfaces for digital collections. Access interfaces depend on the content organization and storage and serve as the bridge between internal (technical services) and user services.

1.3.6. Maintenance

Maintaining buildings and systems and preserving content are important and costly activities in physical libraries. Digital libraries may avoid some of the cost of wear and tear on buildings and books but still have significant maintenance costs, including some unique to electronic environments. New equipment, improved or alternative networks solutions (e.g. ISDN, ATM, Wireless), and software upgrades will require excellent technical personnel. Archivists have long worried about the persistence of digital media. Magnetic tape life expectancies are typically less than ten years under ideal temperature and humidity conditions. Optical storage offers longer life spans, but digital librarians must plan for copying digital holdings periodically and specially for the inevitable obsolescences of different media types and playback devices. These maintenance issues correspond to traditional maintenance requirements, but they apply across many industries and require rapidly changing technical skills, which tend to be much expensive. Just as the computational system change, digital content may also change. A digital document may have numerous versions, especially given the ease with which electronic documents may have changed. Maintaining the most essential document requires that versions be well managed, which includes updating and deleting the links to those objects. In addition to this version control problem, digital librarians must manage the multiplicity of indexes and file formats. Requirements for link managements are more problematic, as hypertext links are created among distinct documents. Although much research and development efforts in digital libraries have been devoted to maintaining the content, but further improvements are required to maintain security, updating versions, tools for automatically checking links, database tools for property rights, etc. for the smooth library functions and services.

1.3.7. Rights Management

Intellectual property right and information security and authority are two global interdependent issues, which influence research and development in digital libraries. Copyright exists to promote intellectual production by providing economic incentives. Security protects unauthorized access as well as ensures the veracity and authority of digital information objects. The misuse that can be put to digital content is far more serious and voluminous than for printed content.. There are various legal issues that make management difficult for digital content. The legal and related issues include: what does it mean to use intellectual property; how can its fair use apply to digital objects; how and whether it may be represented in machine readable form; how, by whom and in what conditions it may be used; how it protects against illegal use, etc. The efforts have been made to change copy right laws to protect the illegal use of digital objects. And also to develop technical solutions that protects copyright either through copy protection or automatic billing mechanism. Research on encryption algorithms, digital watermarking and electronic commerce are leading to the development of trusted system that protect intellectual property rights by managing the necessary financial transactions while protecting consumers by providing authoritative information securely. These techniques ensure the veracity of an object and may help to prevent copying and distribution in an open marketplace.

1.4. FILE FORMAT

File format is one of the core issues in any digital preservation approach. Digital information is produced in a variety of standard and proprietary formats, including ASCII, common image formats, word processing, spreadsheets, database documents, formulae, charts, multimedia files and sound and video. As a result of such a heterogeneous nature of storable information, a high number of file formats are now spread, and many of them often need specific software to view or edit the file. These formats arecontinuously evolving and becoming more complex due to new features and functionality. Before preserving digital records it is necessary to know in which file format the digital record is created. For example, to view an older word processing file, one needs software that understands the encoding schemes of the original software and can display that properly on the screen. Thus several factors need to be considered while adding any document in digital repository.

What is File Format?

Digital information can be saved on any medium that is able to represent the binary digits ("bits") 0 and 1. The meaningful sequence of bits with no intervening spaces, punctuation or formatting is called as bit stream. A file is nothing more than a sequence of bits and the file format is nothing but interpreting the bit stream. Retrieving a bit stream requires a hardware device, such as disk drive and special circuitry for reading the physical representation of the bits from the medium. After a bit stream is retrieved, it must still be interpreted. For interpreting a bit stream the implicit structure of the format needs to be known. Since a disk drive, or any other computer storage system, can only store bits, the computer must have a way to convert information in zeros and ones and vice versa. There are different kinds of formats for different kinds of information (Rothenberg, 1995). The first thing a file format specifies is whether the file is binary or ASCII, and second is how information is organized. Brown (2006) defined file format as 'the internal structure and encoding of a digital object, which allows it to be processed, or to be rendered in human accessible form. A digital object may be a file, or a bit stream embedded within a file'. Different file formats specify how binary digits represent the intellectual content created by a digital object's author. An example of which is the Microsoft Word Format. Microsoft word format is a specification for the storage of textual data, along with formatting information. In order to understand the Microsoft Word Format, software is required to interpret and display the data for the user. Thus there are several file formats which are available today which are incredibly complex, making the binary code meaningless to a human observer if the required software is not available to interpret the format. The aim of digital preservation is ensuring that records are filed and made accessible throughout time, but as a result of progress in software and hardware technology old formats soon become unreadable and unusable. Different research initiatives are focusing on this issue, trying to define preservation-friendly standard formats, as well as strategies for records to be made available over time. There are many initiatives are taken place to read and convert old file formats.

1.4.1. Types of File Formats

There are different categories of file formats available today for different applications. The official categorization of file formats is the MIME type, provided by IANA. They define the following main categories of formats:

- application
- audio
- image
- message
- model

- multipart
- text
- video

Here are a few examples of different file formats used for different applications.

Text files	Images
Word Documents (DOC) Rich Text Format (RTF)	Bitmap (BMP) files Computer Graphics Metafile (CGM) Drawing Interchange Format (DXF) Encapsulated PostScript (EPS) files Joint Photographic Experts Group (JPEG) Graphics Interchange Format (GIF) Tagged Image File Format (TIFF) Portable Network Graphics (PNG)
Audio	**Video**
MPEG layer 3 (MP3) WAVE (WAV) Musical instrument digital interface (MIDI)	Movie (MOV) Windows Media Video (WMV) Audio Video Interleave (AVI) Flash (SWF) QuickTime Virtual Reality (QTVR) QuickTime Movie (MOV)
Spreadsheet	**Databases**
Excel (XLS)	Microsoft Database (MDB)
Presentation	**Markup Languages**
PowerPoint (PPT, PPS) *Portable Document Format (PDF)* files	(HTML, HTM, SGML, XHML, XML)

Compression	Other
Zone Information Protocol (ZIP)	Executable (EXE)

1.4.2. Challenges in Digital File Formats

1. Many file formats become obsolete due to several reasons such as
    - Developer of that file format goes out of business
    - Developer stops supporting that format
    - The market share of the developer declines
    - Supporting program of the software change significantly

- Third party support is lacking etc. (A well known example is WordPerfect file format.)

2. Format depends on obsolete hardware or operating system.
3. Format is proprietary.
4. New versions of application software may not support earlier format versions.
5. Most application software developers produce file format documentation for the formats they design and develop. Not all of them make this documentation available and even if they do, it is not always accurate.
6. The number of file formats is incredibly high. The File Extension collection asserts they have indexed over 15,000 file name extensions (Guercio, 2004).
7. There are many public domain format sites such as My File Formats, Wotsit's Format, File Formats Encyclopedia etc. but they lack any vision or plan to sustain over long period on Internet.
8. Word processing and desktop publishing systems dominate the market for the creation of documents with complex structure and layout, and the software for such use typically models and stores document structure and layout in proprietary terms. Although the software may provide mechanisms for converting documents to common interchange formats, use of such mechanisms often results in the loss or inadequate rendering of content such as page structures and layout of headers, footers and section headings.

1.4.3. File Format Specifications

A file format specification indicates the proper sub division, encoding, sequence, arrangement, size, and internal relationships that uniquely identify the particular format and allow it to be properly interpreted and rendered. For example, a format specification indicates the location of meaningful boundaries within the bit stream and whether a particular subunit should be interpreted as an ASCII character, a numerical value, a machine instruction, a color selection, or something else. Without a format specification a file is just a meaningless sequence of 0s and 1s. Whenever a file is saved, the internal representation of the text document is converted to its standard format. Inversely, when the file is read by another tool, the format is abstracted and converted into its internal representation. Hence it is necessary to know the syntactical and semantic specifications of any digital file. A format specification provides the details necessary to construct a valid file of a particular type and to develop software applications that can decode and render such files (Digital Preservation Online Tutorial, 2004). The actual specifications of any file format may vary considerably in length, from 100 pages to over 1000, depending on the complexity of the format. In digital preservation activities it is necessary to know internal structure of any file. For example, TIFF file format grew from 37 tags in version 4 to 74 tags in version 6.0. New proprietary tags for TIFF version 6.0 are registered with Adobe, which does not make their specification available in public. File format specifications are very important in digital preservation activities. If internal structure of a file is known it is easy to maintain the file in current file format.

1.4.4. File Format Registries

A format registry is a repository for format specification information or, in other words, descriptive, administrative, and technical metadata about digital formats, including the definition of the syntactic and semantic characteristics of the registered formats. This metadata defines the significant properties of digital formats with regard to the long-term preservation of digital objects. Brown (2004) defined file format registries as authoritative and publicly available source of technical information, supporting identification, accession, preservation, and access of files. File format registries are expected to be persistent, trustworthy, and publicly discoverable. The most well-known example of a format registry is the Internet Assigned Names Authority (IANA) MIME type registry. However, MIME registry does not prescribe any specific set of format attributes that must be disclosed. For example, the MIME type application/ msword by itself doesn't help to determine whether a file is compatible with Microsoft Word 6.0 or 2000. Also MIME typing does not provide sufficient granularity to disambiguate important format distinctions, whether based on versioning or profiling. For example, the entire PDF family - PDF 1.0 through 1.4, PDF/ X-1 through 3 (ISO 15930), and the proposed PDF/ A standard - are all typed with a single identifier: application/ pdf. (*www.iana.org/assignments/media-types/*).

A number of projects are investigating or developing systems which provide repositories of file format and representation information for use in digital preservation. The popular format registries are PRONOM, and the future GDFR which provide detailed information about internal specifications of file formats and tools required to render the format.

1.5. PRONOM SERVICES

PRONOM was launched during February 2004 by the digital preservation department of the UK National Archives (http:/ / www.nationalarchives.gov.uk/ pronom/). It is a file format registry. It is an information system about data file formats and their supporting software products needed to open them. It is a web enabled database of information on file formats and their technical dependencies, including hardware, software and operating systems. The task of preserving digital objects requires a reliable, sustained repository of file format information. PRONOM is being made available as an information resource for anyone who needs authoritative information about software products, their support lifecycles and technical requirements, and about the file formats which they support. The PRONOM system developed by PRO captures information about tools used for generating, manipulating, and rendering objects on a per-format basis (Abrams, 2003). It contains 550 file format descriptions as of February 1st, 2004, but does not allow direct access to any specifications they may have stored (Clausen, 2004). The most important propriety of the file PRONOM format registry is the persistence to act as a resource which a digital repository can actually point to (Guercio, 2004).

1.5.1. Global Digital Format Registry

Detailed knowledge of the internal properties of digital formats is necessary to interpret properly the full information content of digital objects. All digital repositories need to be able to identify, validate, characterize and process those objects on a format-specific basis. Digital format representation information is of potential use to all institutions and individuals engaged in digital preservation. Harvard University and the Massachusetts Institute of Technology are leading an initiative to establish a centralized registry of file format information. The initiative is currently at an early stage but has already seen international interest and contribution from a range of institutions and organisations facing digital preservation problems. (*http://hul.harvard.edu/gdfr/*)

Global Digital Format Repository (GDFR) will function as a sustainable public service for the collection, maintenance, and dissemination of authoritative information about the significant syntactic and semantic properties of digital formats and of systems that support and manipulate those formats. GDFR was conceived of as a single centralized repository of format representation information. The scope of GDFR is to "maintain persistent, unambiguous bindings between identifiers for digital formats and representation for those formats". The GDFR will function as the persistent memory of the digital preservation community to ensure that the format knowledge often taken for granted today will remain accessible to the community in future. The main objective of registry is to support a range of preservation functions such as:

1. Automatic identification of file formats – given a digital object; what format is it?
2. Verification of digital objects compliance to a relevant file format specification - given an object that is supposed to be of format F; is it?
3. Delivery - given an object of format F; how can it be rendered?
4. Transformation – given an object of format F, to what formats can it be converted to?
5. Risk assessment – given an object of format type F; is it at risk of obsolescence?
6. Characterization - Given a format F; what are the representation specifications of F?

1.5.2. Classifications of File Formats

Proprietary formats : Proprietary formats are licensed and their full documentation is not always available. The user cannot modify the format freely. Their license agreement gets changed. There may be restrictions for using and modifying any proprietary file formats. In proprietary formats their format code sequence is not available to the end user.

Open formats : Open formats are always fully documented, they are not licensed, and the user can freely modify the format structure. One can use open formats for unlimited period. There are no license fees for open formats and there are no patent owners for open formats as well as their full documentation is available permanently. One can also make modifications in these formats.

1.5.3. Recommendation of Using File Formats in Digital Libraries

It is necessary to consider the following principles while creating any digital document in any format to make the format available for the long term such as (Christensen, 2004):

- The format should be simple to describe, understand and implement
- The format should not depend on specific hardware
- The format should not depend on specific operating systems
- The format should not depend on proprietary software
- The format should be robust against single points of failure

In the digital library literature that are many contributions that suggest which are the file formats more appropriate for preservation issue. The preferred formats should be those that remain usable for a significant amount of time. Four types of basic file formats are considered within the digital library communities: text, image, sound and video and for each categories specific standard format are suggested as described in the table below. These formats can be referred to as preferred formats as they will remain usable over a significant amount of time (Guercio, 2004).

Type of file	Format suggested
Text	Unicode (ASCII), XML and PDF/A, ODF (Open Document Format)
Image	Raster: standard TIFF for master copies(no-compression, high resolution), JPEG for safety copies or distribution, PNG (Portable Network Graphics) Vector: CGM, EPS, DXF, SVG
Sound	Compressionless WAV (PCM-coding)
Video	MPEG, OMF (Open Media Framework)

XML (eXtensible Markup Language) is now accepted as the universal format for data and document exchange, and has actually become the lingua franca of the Information Age. XML shows the great promise of data longevity (or future proofing), in a situation in which hardware, software, and network protocols continue to change. XML and PDF are often presented as the two rival formats, with the idea that if you wish to preserve a record long-term you should choose one of the two. PDF and XML are complementary to the point that, in terms of preservation, it is actually better to use them both, rather than choose one of the two. And actually, choosing both standards is also a way of 'sharing the risk': if within a hundred years one of the two formats will no longer be readable, the other might still be so. PDF cannot be used as an archival format hence long term solutions are needed to keep digital PDF records accessible for a long time length. The PDF/A format have been expressly introduced for the purpose. In order to satisfy preservation criteria the PDF/A attempts to achieve the objectives of device independence, self-containment, and self-documentation. Self-containment is defined as the degree to which a PDF/A file may contain all the necessary resources for performing interpretation and rendering in a reliable way and as expected to, while self-documentation is defined as the degree to which a PDF/A file would document itself in terms of descriptive, administrative, structural, and technical metadata.

1.6. AMERICAN STANDARD CODE FOR INFORMATION INTERCHANGE (ASCII)

American Standard Code for Information Interchange (ASCII) is a character encoding based on the English alphabet. ASCII codes represent text in computers, communications equipment, and other devices that work with text. Most modern character encodings which support many more characters than did the original have a historical basis in ASCII. Work on ASCII began in 1960. The first edition of the standard was published in 1963 a major revision in 1967, and in 1986. It currently defines codes for 128 characters where 33 are non-printing, and 94 are printable characters (excluding the space).

Like other character encodings, ASCII specifies a correspondence between digital bit patterns and character symbols (i.e. graphemes and control characters). This allows digital devices to communicate with each other and to process, store, and communicate character-oriented information such as written language. The ASCII character encoding is used on nearly all common computers, especially personal computers and workstations. The preferred MIME name for this encoding is "US-ASCII". ASCII does not define any mechanism for describing the structure or appearance of text within a document.

ASCII is, strictly, a seven-bit code, meaning it uses patterns of seven binary digits (a range of 0 to 127 decimal) to represent each character. When ASCII was introduced, many computers used eight-bit bytes (groups of bits), also called octets, as the native data type. In seven-bit ASCII encoding, the eighth bit was commonly used as a parity bit for error checking on communication lines or for other device-specific functions. Machines that did not use parity checking typically set the eighth bit to 0.

1.6.1. ASCII Control Characters

ASCII reserves the first 32 codes (numbers 0-31 decimal) for control characters; these are codes originally intended not to carry printable information, but rather to control devices (such as printers) that make use of ASCII, or to provide metainformation about data streams such as those stored on magnetic tape. For example, character 10 represents the "line feed" function, character 8 represents "backspace", and the character 13 represents the "carriage return".

1.6.2. ASCII Printable Characters

The code 32, the "space" character, denotes the space between words, as produced by the space-bar of a keyboard. The codes 33 to 126, known as the printable characters, represent letters, digits, punctuation marks, and a few miscellaneous symbols. Table 2.1 shows the ASCII character space that includes both control (0-31) and printable (32-127) characters.

	0	1	2	3	4	5	6	7	8	9
0	NUL	SOH	STX	ETX	EOT	ENQ	ACK	BEL	BS	HT
10	LF	VT	FF	CR	SO	SI	DLE	DC1	DC2	DC3
20	DC4	NAK	SYN	ETB	CAN	EM	SUB	ESC	FS	GS
30	RS	US	SP	!	"	#	$	%	&	'
40	(	)	*	+	,	-	.	/	0	1
50	2	3	4	5	6	7	8	9	:	;
60	<	=	>	?	@	A	B	C	D	E
70	F	G	H	I	J	K	L	M	N	O
80	P	Q	R	S	T	U	V	W	X	Y
90	Z	[	\	]	^	_	`	a	b	c
100	d	e	f	g	h	i	j	k	l	m
110	n	o	p	q	r	s	t	u	v	w
120	x	y	z	{	|	}	~	Del		

ASCII Character Space

1.6.3. ASCII Fits In

ASCII stands for "American Standard Code for Information Interchange" and was created by the American Standards Association (later renamed the American National Standards Institute).

The ASCII standard was started in 1960 and released in 1963. It was an extension of telegraphic codes and was first used by Bell data services.

Major revisions were made over the years. Until 2007 it was the most widely used character encoding on the web, but it was replaced with UTF-8.

The web's switch from ASCII and Microsoft's ANSI towards UTF-8 can be largely attributable to initiatives by

Google, as internet usage was becoming more international and ASCII was only capable of displaying Latin characters.

What's important to note, is that UTF-8 is a type of encoding, while Unicode is the character set; because Unicode's first 128 characters are the same as ASCII, it is acceptable to refer to an ASCII table when generating characters in HTML.

ASCII does have the ability to use an "escape sequence" in displaying alternative alphabets, which allowed it to become an international standard, but Unicode handles this more directly.

Unicode originated from Apple in 1987, and became the project of the Unicode Consortium in 1991. ASCII was created by the ASA, but further refinement of it continued as part of declarations from ISO.

The encoding name of UTF-8 is used by all the standards conforming to the Internet Assigned Numbers Authority (IANA) which means all HTML, CSS, and XML. IANA is a department of the larger ICANN, which is the non-profit which determines internet protocol and domain names.

To summarize, ASCII evolved from telegraph code in the 60's, grew up, and became part of the Unicode character set, which is used by UTF-8, the most dominant encoding format on the web.

Domain names and webpage code depend on having this unified character map to work properly.

This means that at the very root of the modern internet, there exists a character format invented in the 1870's, computerized as ASCII in the 1960's, modernized for the web with Unicode the 1990's, and broadly adopted through UTF-8's majority use in 2007.

1.6.4. Control Characters vs Printable Characters

There are two types of characters in ASCII, printable characters and control characters.

The control characters define numbers 0-31, and 127. The control characters include all the parts of writing that allow for new paragraphs, tabs, end of lines, file separators, and a lot of pieces which are mainly transparent.

These control characters were created at a time when printed cards were a big part of the computing process. Some of those features have since been replaced, but a lot of the line formatting parts are still around today. Code 127 is actually the code for delete (only in real ASCII, not ANSI or Unicode).

All of the printable characters are what you might expect. There are all the lower case characters (a-z) and uppercase characters (A-Z), along with numbers, symbols, and punctuation marks – essentially everything seen on a typical keyboard. These principle characters comprise all written words.

1.6.5. Using ASCII in XML and HTML

Every HTML page has a character encoding format assigned to it.

Unless otherwise specified, the HTML encoding will default to UTF-8. For using pure ASCII, or ANSI, or any specialized, unique format, all that needs to be done is to have a declaration in a meta tag.

For HTML 4:

<meta http-equiv="Content-Type" content="text/html;charset=ISO-8859-1">

For HTML5:

<meta charset="UTF-8">

In the charset tag, you can use UTF-8, ANSI, or ASCII by using charset="us-ascii" or you could look up a specific character set to use, usually by declaring an ISO number. A full list can be found on the IANA character sets page.

1.6.6. Character Code Insertion Format

Generally, however, when someone refers to using the ASCII code, you will want them to clarify if they mean TRUE US-ASCII with a meta-tag, or if they are just asking you to display a special character.

In HTML, any time you want to use a special character, like say the cent symbol (¢) or an inverted question mark character (¿) – you would generally be able to use a Unicode symbol or US-ASCII (8-bit) character, by typing in a reference like this:

¢ in HTML looks like: ¢

¿ in HTML looks like: ¿

So you start with an &# followed by a four-digit number, finishing with a semi-colon (;).

In this way, you are able to display characters based on their ASCII/Unicode number.

Of course, control characters will perform a formatting function or not work at all, depending on which one you use and which real character set you have listed in your meta tag.

So in HTML you see the "&#" number, but when displayed in your browser you will see the character.

1.7. HTML SPECIAL ENTITY CHARACTERS

Now, let's say for example you want to just show an & symbol on your page.

You can't just type it into the HTML, but you can type in the corresponding ASCII or Unicode.

HTML is a markup language, so while normal letters work fine, special characters and especially <> brackets – are critically important to how the browser reads and shows the HTML.

You don't need to always type in the Unicode/ASCII reference number though. For HTML 4.0 and newer, there are special entities which work similar to a Unicode reference, but instead of memorizing a number you memorize a word.

¢ in HTML looks like: ¢

¿ in HTML looks like: ¿

A full list of these character references can be found at the W3 consortium.

Reference Table : With all this lead-up, you might just be looking for an easy place to find an ASCII or Unicode reference. Look no further, we have references 000-127 here, and you can find the full Unicode format on Wikipedia.

Note that characters 000-032 and 127 are not generally printable and are thus indicated with "NA."

ASCII

```
table.wiht002 {
border-spacing: 0px;
border-collapse:collapse;
margin-left: auto;
margin-right: auto;
margin-bottom: 1.5em;
text-align: center;
}
table, tr, td
{
padding: 0px;
margin: 0px;
}
td.bor
{
border-left: 1px solid #000;
padding-left: 1em;
```

```
margin-right: 1em;
}
td.break
{
margin-left: 2em;
margin-right: 2em;
}
td.sep
{
border-bottom: 1px solid #000;
}
td.sepbor
{
border-bottom: 1px solid #000;
border-left: 1px solid #000;
padding-left: 1em;
margin-right: 1em;
}
```

0	NA	&#0000;	32	NA		64	@	@	96	‘	‘
1	NA	&#0001;	33	!	!	65	A	A	97	a	a
2	NA	&#0002;	34	“	“	66	B	B	98	b	b
3	NA	&#0003;	35	#	#	67	C	C	99	c	c
4	NA	&#0004;	36	$	$	68	D	D	100	d	d
5	NA	&#0005;	37	%	%	69	E	E	101	e	e
6	NA	&#0006;	38	&	&	70	F	F	102	f	f
7	NA	&#0007;	39	‘	‘	71	G	G	103	g	g
8	NA	&#0008;	40	(	(	72	H	H	104	h	h
9	NA		41	)	)	73	I	I	105	i	i
10	NA		42	*	*	74	J	J	106	j	j
11	NA	&#0011;	43	+	+	75	K	K	107	k	k
12	NA		44	,	,	76	L	L	108	l	l

13	NA		45	-	-	77	M	M	109	m	m
14	NA	&#0014;	46	.	.	78	N	N	110	n	n
15	NA	&#0015;	47	/	/	79	O	O	111	o	o
16	NA	&#0016;	48	0	0	80	P	P	112	p	p
17	NA	&#0017;	49	1	1	81	Q	Q	113	q	q
18	NA	&#0018;	50	2	2	82	R	R	114	r	r
19	NA	&#0019;	51	3	3	83	S	S	115	s	s
20	NA	&#0020;	52	4	4	84	T	T	116	t	t
21	NA	&#0021;	53	5	5	85	U	U	117	u	u
22	NA	&#0022;	54	6	6	86	V	V	118	v	v
23	NA	&#0023;	55	7	7	87	W	W	119	w	w
24	NA	&#0024;	56	8	8	88	X	X	120	x	x
25	NA	&#0025;	57	9	9	89	Y	Y	121	y	y
26	NA	&#0026;	58	:	:	90	Z	Z	122	z	z
27	NA	&#0027;	59	;	;	91	[	[	123	{	{
28	NA	&#0028;	60	<	<	92	\	\	124	|	|
29	NA	&#0029;	61	=	=	93	]	]	125	}	}
30	NA	&#0030;	62	>	>	94	^	^	126	~	~
31	NA	&#0031;	63	?	?	95	_	_	127	NA	n

1.7.1. ASCII Tools and Resources

There is a lot of history on how character codes evolved, and the organizations which hold these standards together for the rest of us. With most internet developers and the W3C settling on UTF-8, for at least the immediate future, that is how pages will be encoded.

You're going to need some resources to help you though if you start manually encoding in other formats, or it can be nice just to have a comprehensive reference around.

ASCII Art : No summary of ASCII would be complete without a reference to ASCII art.

Special software can be used, or symbols hand-coded, to take on the shape of an image using nothing but symbols. This type of effect has existed since the 1980s and made popular on systems like the Commodore Amiga Computer.

There is even a distinction between "Oldskool" ASCII art which uses pure ASCII in the command line, and "Newskool" which uses the special characters in Unicode to make even more complex works of art.

Here's a picture of a zebra's head:

1.8. UNICODE

Unicode is a standard for character encoding managed by The Unicode Consortium.

As we've discussed, computer systems don't store characters (letters, numbers, symbols) literally — there's no tiny picture of each letter in a document on your hard drive. As you should now know, each character is encoded as a series of binary bits — 1s and 0s. For example, the code for the lowercase letter "a" is 01100001.

But 01100001 is arbitrary — there's nothing special about that string of bits that should make it the letter "a" — the computer industry has collectively agreed that it means "a." So how does the entire industry come to agree on how to represent every possible character? With a character encoding standard. An encoding standard simply specifies all the possible characters available, and assigns each one a string of bits.

There has been several character encoding standards used around the world over the last several decades of computing. For a long time, the most universally-accepted standard was ASCII. The problem with ASCII is that it only encoded a relatively limited number of characters — 256 at most. This excluded non-Latin languages, many important math and science symbols, and even some basic punctuation marks.

Aside from ASCII's use in English and other languages which use the Latin alphabet, language groups using other alphabets tended to use their own character encoding. Since these encoding schemes were defined apart from each other, they often conflicted; it was impossible to use a single encoding scheme for multiple languages at the same time.

Unicode was originally conceived, and continues to be developed, specifically with the intent to overcome these challenges. The goal of Unicode is to provide a uniersal, unified, and unique code identifier for every grapheme in every language and writing system in the world.

UTF-8 : Unicode has been implemented in several character encoding schemes, but the standard most widely used today is UTF-8. UTF-8 has become nearly universal for all types of modern computing.

UTF-8 encodes characters using up to 4 8-bit code blocks. ASCII only used 8 bits per character. Unicode characters previously included in ASCII are represented in UTF-8 by a single 8-bit chunk, the same 8 bits that were used in ASCII. This makes ASCII text forward-compatible in UTF-8. (This is one of the many reasons that UTF-8 became the universal standard — transition was relatively easy.)

The 8×4 scheme provides UTF-8 with over a million code points, allowing Unicode to encode characters from 129 scripts and writing systems.

1.8.1. Resources for Understanding Unicode

- An Introduction to Writing Systems and Unicode is a very thorough, even eloquent, explanation of character encoding generally, and Unicode in particular; if you can only read one thing on Unicode, this is the one to read
- The Unicode Standard: A Technical Introduction is the official explanation of the Unicode standard
- To the BMP and Beyond! is a tutorial on Unicode, suitable for classrom presentation or self-study
- The Unicode Tutorial explains how Unicode works, including interesting details like combining characters, and how a Unicode parsing engine should function.

1.8.2. Books on Unicode

- Unicode Explained, by JukkaKorpela, provides a good overview of Unicode and various development challenges that come with implementing it
- Unicode Demystified: A Practical Programmer's Guide to the Encoding Standard, by Richard Gillam, is a helpful, if somewhat dated, explanation of Unicode, with a lot of Java-focused implementation specifics
- Fonts and Encodings, by YannisHaralambous, is not solely about Unicode, but might be the book most worth reading; it covers the history of encoding and representing text in computers, providing both a theoretical and practical foundation for understanding Unicode and a number of closely related subjects.

1.8.3. Unicode Reference Material

Once you have a basic understanding of Unicode, you'll mostly find yourself needing to look up specific details – such as the exact encoding of a particular character.

- The C/C++ Unicode Cheatsheet provides info on converting Microsoft C/C++ to Unicode

- XML and Unicode Technology Reports is a list of technical reports covering various aspects of using XML and Unicode together
- Decode Unicode provides an online Unicode dictionary with a beautiful UI, allowing you to view every defined Unicode character, even without local font support
- Data on Languages provides searchable information on using Unicode character sets with various languages
- Unicode Navigator provides an organized list of all the Unicode characters

1.8.4. Unicode Tools

- Unicode Analyzer is a Chrome browser extension that provides information on Unicode text in web pages and documents
- Character Identifier is a Firefox plugin that provides a context menu for finding more information about selected Unicode characters
- For inserting Unicode characters in text fields on the web, try Unicode Symbols for Chrome or Unicode Input Tool for Firefox
- UnicodeDataBrowser provides a GUI for easier reading of the UnicodeData.txt file
- Polyglot 3000 automatically identifies the language of any text
- Unicode provides a list of Unicode character keyboard layouts for various Unicode-supported scripts
- Babel is a Python library for a wide range of internationalization and localization tasks
- D-Type Unicode Text Engine is a C++ library for laying out, rendering, and editing high-quality Unicode text on any device, platform, or operating system
- Nunicode is a C library for encoding and decoding of UTF-8 documents

- Portable UTF-8 provides Unicode support for PHP strings
- Tesseract OCR provides optical character recognition for Unicode text
- Popchar is an improved character map that lets you easily find and type characters from the whole range of the Unicode space
- Unicode Utilities provides a number of interesting and useful online tools for working with Unicode
- Edicode provides an flexible online Unicode keyboard for typing text using various international scripts
- Quickkey is a flexible keyboard extension for typing the first 65,000 defined Unicode characters
- Unicode Code Converter converts any entered character code into several different encodings of the same character
- CharFunk is a JavaScript utility for performing a number of interesting checks and operations on Unicode characters
- Kreative Recode transforms text files from various encoding into Unicode
- BabelMap Online provides an in-browser Unicode keyboard, with output in display characters as well as hex or decimal encoding

1.8.5. Text and Code Editors

Most of today's text editors, code editors, and IDEs either use Unicode by default, or can easily handle Unicode. Sublime, Notepad++, Atom, and Eclipse are all set to UTF-8 as the default character encoding. Vim and Emacs may need a setting change to use UTF-8:

- Using Unicode with Emacs
- Using Unicode with Vim

There are also a handful of code and text editors specifically designed to handle the extended Unicode character set:

- MinEd is a Unicode text editor with contextual support for inserting characters from the full range of the Unicode character space
- Classical Text Editor is an advanced editor for working with critical and scholarly editions of texts, including multi-lingual texts using a wide range of the Unicode character set

1.8.6. Unicode Fonts

The relationship between fonts and Unicode is a bit oblique. Unicode was created to be backward-compatible with ASCII — text formatted in ASCII can be decoded as Unicode with virtually no problem. And Unicode-encoded text can be displayed using ASCII fonts, as long as only the small set of characters that appear in ASCII are used.

Today, most fonts available on most computers are encoded with Unicode. So, from that standpoint, most fonts are "Unicode fonts." However, most fonts do not support a particularly large set of the full Unicode standard.

Usually, this is not a problem; someone authoring a text in multiple languages, or with an extended character set, might use several different fonts — one for Latin script, another for each CJK languages, and another for math symbols (for example). However, it can be useful sometimes to have single fonts which contain a large percentage of the Unicode character space. This might be needed when working in plain text and source code environments where using multiple fonts is not feasible, or when visual unity between multiple scripts is especially important.

The following are the most notable font projects providing extended Unicode support. For a more complete listing, including defunct and deprecated fonts, see this page of Unicode fonts. For typesetting Asian languages, see this list of CJK fonts.

- Everson Mono is a monospace font created by one of the originators of the Unicode standard; its stated purpose is to provide glyphs for as much of the Unicode character space as possible, and (as of this writing) 92 Unicode character blocks are supported.Noto is a large set of display fonts, developed by Google, which together provide support for a high majority of the Unicode character sets, with the intention to eventually support the entire Unicode standard.
- Deja Vu Fonts is a font family providing wide coverage of the Unicode standard, with Serif, Sans, and Monospace versions.
- GNU FreeFont is a family of fonts, providing Serif, Sans, and Mono type faces for 37 writing systems and 12 Unicode symbol ranges.
- GNU Unifont is a monospace, bitmap font with complete coverage for the Unicode 8.0 Basic Multilingual Plane and wide, but incomplete, coverage for the Supplemental Multilingual Plane.

There are also a number of interesting fonts which encode a particular subset of the Unicode standard for specialized use.

- Unicode is a set of fonts for Medievalists
- Last Resort is a "font of last resort"; instead of conventional character glyphs, each glyph actually displays information about the Unicode character itself
- Unicode Fonts for Ancient Scripts is a project to create a set of fonts for several ancient and classical alphabets
- Unimath Plus provides an extended set of science and math symbols

And here are some additional Unicode font resources, if you still can't find what you are looking for:

- SIL Fonts a number of fonts for various under-supported languages, created by SIL International, a global non-profit serving minority language communities
- Unicode character ranges and the Unicode fonts that support them will help you find a font for any range of Unicode characters.

1.9. INDIAN SCRIPT CODE FOR INFORMATION INTERCHANGE (ISCII)

In the early eighties, the Dept, of Electronics of the Govt, of India set up an expert committee to set up standards for information processing of Indie languages. The Indian script Code for Information Interchange (ISCII), was first launched in 1984, is the outcome of this exercise. The ISCII is an 8-bit umbrella standard, defined in such a way that all Indian languages can be treated using one single character encoding scheme. ISCII is a bilingual character encoding (not glyphs) scheme. Roman characters and punctuation marks as defined in the standard lower-ASCII take up the first half the character set (first 128 slots). Characters for indie languages are allocated to the upper slots (128-255). The Indian Standard ISCII-84 was subsequently revised in 1991 (ISCI1-91) and 1997 (ISCII-97). Along with the character encoding scheme (ISCII), the Govt, of India also defined a keyboard layout for input called INSCRIPT. The research and development wing of the DOE, Govt of India has developed software Commercial DTP packages based on ISCII are also available. ISCII has not been widely used outside of certain government institutions and has now been rendered largely obsolete by Unicode. While using a separate block for each Indie writing system, Unicode largely preserve the ISCII layout within each block. In a 7-bit environment the control code SI can be used for invocation of the ISCII code set, and the control code SO can be used for reselection of the ASCII code set. There are 15 officially recognized languages in India: Hindi, Marathi, Sanskrit,

Punjabi, Gujarati, Oriya, Bengali, Assamese, Telugu, Kannada, Malayalam, Tamil, Urdu, Sindhi and Kashmiri. Out of these, Urdu, Sindhi and Kashmiri are primarily written in Perso-Aabic scripts. Apart from Perso-Arabic scripts, all the other 10 scripts used for Indian languages have evolved from the ancient Brahmi script and have a common phonetic structure, making a common character set possible. The northern scripts are Devanagari, Punjabi, Gujarati, Oriya, Bengali and Assamese, while the southern scripts are Telugu, Kannada, Malayalam and Tamil. The official language of India, Hindi is written in the devanagari script. Devanagari is also used for writing Marathi and Sanskrit. It is also the official script of Nepal. As Perso-Arabic scripts have a different alphabet, a different standard is envisaged for them. An attribute mechanism has been provided for selection of different Indian script font and display attributes. An extension mechanism allows use of more characters along with the ISCII code. The ISCII code table is a super-set of all the characters required in the ten Brahmi-based Indian scripts. The Arabic-based writing systems have subsequently been encoded in the PASCII encoding. The ISCII code standard specifies a 7-bit code table which can be used in 7 or 8-bit ISO compatible packages based on these Indian standards. Multilingual and Multimedia products are based on Graphics and Intelligence-based Script Technology (GIST).

1.10. PROPERTIES OF ISCII CODE

Phonetic Sequence : The ISCII characters, within a word, are kept in the same order as they would get pronounced.

No Direct Sorting: Since there are variations in ordering of a few consonants between different Indian scripts, it is not possible to achieve perfect sorting in all Indian scripts. Special routines would be required.

Unique Spellings: By using only the basic characters in ISCII, there is only one unique way of typing a word.

Display Independence : A word in an Indian script can be displayed in a variety of styles depending on the conjunct repertoire used. ISCII codes however allow a complete delinking of the codes from the displayed fonts. The Inscript keyboard overlay has one-to-one correspondence with the ISCII code. This way, typing of word does not depend upon its displayed form.

Transliteration : The ISCII codes are rendered on the display device according to the display composition methodology of the selected script. Transliteration to another script can thus be obtained by merely redisplaying the same text in a different script. Since the display rendering process can be very flexible, it is possible to transliterate the Indian scripts to the Roman script, using diacritic marks. Similarly it is possible to transliterate them to their scripts such as Perso-Arabic. Transliteration involves mere change of the script, in a manner that pronunciation is not affected. This is not the same as "translation" here the language itself changes. Table shows below the ISCII table for Hindi.

	Hex	0	1	2	3	4	5	6	7	8	9	A	B	C	D	E	F
Hex	Dec	0	16	32	48	64	80	96	112	128	144	160	176	192	208	224	240
0	0	NUL	DLE	SP	0	@	P	`	p				ओ	ढ	ऱ	ॆ	EXT
1	1	SOH	DC1	!	1	A	Q	a	q			ँ	औ	ण	ल	े	०
2	2	STX	DC2	"	2	B	R	b	r			ं	ऑ	त	ळ	ै	१
3	3	ETX	DC3	#	3	C	S	c	s			ः	क	थ	ऴ	ॅ	२
4	4	EOT	DC4	$	4	D	T	d	t			अ	ख	द	व	ॊ	३
5	5	ENQ	NAK	%	5	E	U	e	u			आ	ग	ध	श	ो	४
6	6	ACK	SYN	&	6	F	V	f	v			इ	घ	न	ष	ौ	५
7	7	BEL	ETB	'	7	G	W	g	w			ई	ङ	ऩ	स	ॉ	६
8	8	BS	CAN	(	8	H	X	h	x			उ	च	प	ह	।	७
9	9	HT	EM	)	9	I	Y	i	y			ऊ	छ	फ	INV		८
A	10	LF	SUB	*	:	J	Z	j	z			ऋ	ज	ब	ा		९
B	11	VT	ESC	+	;	K	[	k	{			ऎ	झ	भ	ि		
C	12	FF	FS	,	<	L	\	l	|			ए	ञ	म	ी		
D	13	CR	GS	-	=	M	]	m	}			ऐ	ट	य	ु		
E	14	SO	RS	.	>	N	^	n	~			ऍ	ठ	य़	ू		
F	15	SI	US	/	?	O	_	o	DEL			ऒ	ड	र	ृ	ATR	

ISCII Table For Hindi

1.11. SUMMARY

Today there is a shift in rendering information on the web in different languages. Internet has brought a movement for the globalisation of information. Since the world has great deal of diversity in cultures, languages and scripts, UNICODE has taken up the challenge for the globalisation of world scripts in IT as well as Virtual world (Internet). There are several technical and political constraints in its development. Updations of it are coming from time to time, which include additional and modified rules. Though this standard is an effort of software companies, it has a variety of applications in today's world and libraries stand a better chance for resource sharing

1.12. REVIEW QUESTION

1. Define content type creation and types
2. List and explain Classifications of File Formats
3. Define Unicode Tools

Unit 2

OBJECTIVES

1. To learn about programming languages
2. To implement Markup languages
3. To defined in the HTML document

2.1. INTRODUCTION

The term "markup" originates in the publishing business, where it originally meant the marks that editor, lectors, and printers add to drafts of texts to communicate among themselves about the changes they require to be made to the layout or the structure of a text that is going through the editing process. In computer applications, text markup has acquired the generalized meaning of information added to a text (i.e., information that does not appear in print) which describes the logical structure of the text (chapters, sections), defines aspects of the layout of the text (bold-face, page break), or which contains lightly structured information about the text (author, date published, ISBN). These three types of markup have been known in the text markup literature as structural markup, specific markup, and meta data, respectively. The ISO standard SGML (Standard Generalized Markup Language) was designed for use by publishers to replace their paper-and-pencil based document designs and document markings within a computerized environment. SGML allowed the definition of extremely complex Document Types (DTDs) that specify the logical structures available for documents of its type and their syntactic representation in these documents; such DTDs would then be compiled into parsers and processors for text documents of the specified type. Due to its staggering complexity, SGML never became widely used outside big publishing houses, despite such grandiose efforts as those of the Text Encoding Initiative. Instead, a few simple DTDs eventually became widely used without explicit reference to their SGML DTD as the World Wide Web began its explosive development over the last decade. Thus, the term "Markup" as used in the heading of this section of the paper is best known today as the "M" in "HTML" – the hypertext markup language. Few people have ever bothered to look at actual DTDs for HTML, even though HTML was meant to work as an SGML application. Instead, the very simple syntax defined in the

HTML document type was typically written and interpreted directly without the help of a generic SGML tool. Nevertheless, HTML is today "the" prototypical example for the term "Markup" as it offers descriptors for the logical structuring of documents (headers, paragraphs, crossreferences), for layout control (bold face, tables), and even for marking editorial changes (strike through). A more recent addition to HTML is actually an integral part of the concept of text markup: style sheets that map the logical structure of a document to a screen or paper layout that visualizes that structure to a reader. This is an important development as it helps separate the logical structure from its realization in the form of specific printing conventions.

2.2. MARKUP LANGUAGE

Thus, a Markup Language comes in several parts: a language that is used when defining a document type (that is, for writing DTDs1), a language for the markup that encodes the logical structure of a document according to such a DTD, and a way to intermix the markup with the plain text of a document while retaining the ability to distinguish between markup and text. Recently, there has been a huge effort in the software and Internet industry to develop a simplified SGML for use on the Web, dubbed XML for "eXtensible Markup Language". XML provides the basic syntactic framework for a whole family of more or less closely related languages. Core XML provides the basic syntactic features for container or empty elements with attributes and attribute values, Unicode text and entities, and comments, DTDs, and processing instructions. The XML effort includes a large number of ongoing projects to add more standard functionality and usefulness to the basic syntactic framework of XML, such as style sheets (XSL), cross-referencing (XLink, XPointer), name spaces, embedding of XML fragments in other XML documents (XML Schemas), to name just a few. Much of this is being done in the form of projects of the World Wide Web

Consortium in conjunction with the software industry.

2.3. DIFFERENCE BETWEEN PROGRAMMING, SCRIPTING, AND MARKUP LANGUAGES

When it comes to making a website or app coding involves basically three types of languages i.e the programming language, Scripting Language and Markup Language.

There are a lot of people who consider coding as just developing or making a website but they need to understand every single language fits into a particular category and we need to know which category that language fits into. We will discuss in detail about the difference between these three main categories or pillars of a website or an app i.e. Programming language, Scripting Language and Markup Language.

2.4 PROGRAMMING LANGUAGE

In simple terms, programming languages are set of instructions or code which tells a computer what it needs to do. So basically, we provide a logic or instruction to the computer to perform some task to get the desired output from it. When we need to write a CD or burn a CD or when we need to paste something in pen drive these all instruction is given through some software which involves some instructions or set of code and this software communicate to the hardware. Programming languages are high-level languages that need to be converted into machine level language because a computer can only understand machine level language or binary language (0 and 1). So we write the instructions in human-readable form and then we hit the compile button to convert this into machine level language which a computer can understand and then the computer performs the task. This conversion is done by the compiler which scans the complete code in one go and if it finds any error it immediately throws all errors. Examples are *Java, C, C++, C#*. Programming languages are most widely used to make software or drivers.

2.4.1. Scripting Language

As the name suggest, it's all about giving the script to perform some certain task. Scripting languages are basically the subcategory of programming languages which is used to give guidance to another program or we can say to control another program, so it also involves instructions. It basically connects one language to one another languages and doesn't work standalone. *Javascript, PHP, Perl, Python,* VBScript these all are the examples of scripting language. Scripting languages need to be interpreted (Scanning the code line by line, not like compiler in one go) instead of compiled. There is ***no scope of compiler*** in scripting languages. Scripting languages are most widely used to create a website.

2.4.2. Markup Languages

Markup languages are completely different from programming languages and scripting languages. Markup languages prepare a structure for the data or prepare the look or design of a page. These are ***presentational*** languages and it doesn't include any kind of logic or algorithm, for example, HTML. *HTML* is not asking any kind of question to the computer or it's not comparing things and it's not asking any logical question. It's just used to represent a view inside a web browser. It tells the browser how to structure data for a specific page, layout, headings, title, table and all or styling a page in a particular way. So basically it involves formatting data or it controls the presentation of data. Examples of Markup languages are HTML, *CSS* or XML. These languages are most widely used to design a website.

From the above definition, we can summarize Programming language, Scripting language, and Markup languages from below images.

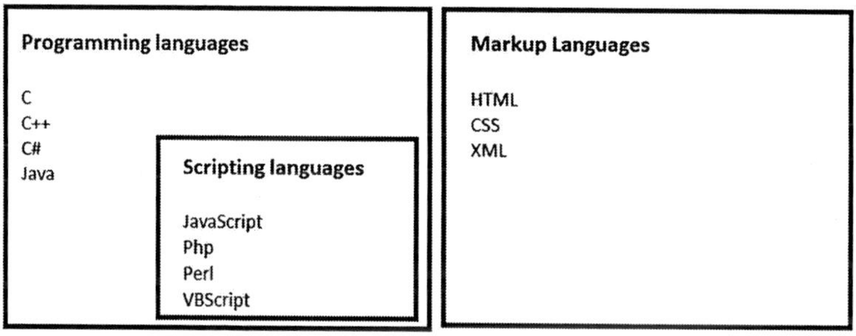

Document markup is a notation method that defines how particular pieces of information are meant to be formatted. The term comes from the practice of marking up manuscripts to notate changes that need to be made. Markup in terms of programming languages is used to identify a language that specifies how a document is to appear.

If you have ever used multiple colors of ink or highlighter when making notes and ascribed meaning to those colors for yourself (e.g., yellow highlighter is important, red ink is a definition) then you have already practiced document markup. You are providing additional layers of information along with the written text, in this case visual cues as to the purpose of the written information.

Some popular markup languages are hypertext markup language (HTML), extensible markup language (XML) and extensible hypertext markup language (XHTML). These were each created to fulfill particular needs in defining the layout and structure of the material.

2.5. SGML (STANDARD GENERALIZED MARKUP LANGUAGE)

SGML (Standard Generalized Markup Language) is a standard for how to specify a document markup language or tag set. Such a specification is itself a document type definition (DTD). SGML is not in itself a document language, but a description of how to specify one. It is metadata.

SGML is based on the idea that documents have structural and other semantic elements that can be described without reference to how such elements should be displayed. The actual display of such a document may vary, depending on the output medium and style preferences. Some advantages of documents based on SGML are:

They can be created by thinking in terms of document structure rather than appearance characteristics (which may change over time).

They will be more portable because an SGML compiler can interpret any document by reference to its document type definition (DTD).

Documents originally intended for the print medium can easily be re-adapted for other media, such as the computer display screen.

The language that this Web browser uses, Hypertext Markup Language (HTML), is an example of an SGML-based language. There is a document type definition for HTML (and reading the HTML specification is effectively reading an expanded version of the document type definition). In today's distributed networking environment, many documents are being described with the Extensible Markup Language (XML) which is a data description language (and a document can be viewed as a collection of data) that uses SGML principles.

SGML is based somewhat on earlier generalized markup languages developed at IBM, including General Markup Language (GML) and ISIL.

SGML (Standard Generalized Markup Language) was first developed in 1970 as GML (Generalized Markup Language) and evolved into both a national and international standard (Bradley, 272). SGML has been an international standard since October 1986 (ISO Standard 8879); it is widely accepted in the United States, Western Europe, and Japan and is used for a variety of business, industrial and academic applications (Adler, 556). SGML is frequently referred to as a meta language. This means that SGML is not a single language, but a language that describes other markup languages; that is, SGML is the rules or framework for defining particular markup languages.

SGML provides for descriptive, as opposed to procedural, markup; that is, it simply states names to categorize parts of a document instead of specifying processes to be carried out.

SGML permits the description of structured information independent of its processing by providing a standard syntax for defining descriptions of classes of documents. These descriptions are called document type definitions (DTDs). DTDs define types of documents and their structures by stating what elements are required in a particular type, and what elements may be present in the document. The structure of a document can be marked up and checked against a DTD – using a special program called a parser – to ensure that it is valid, and that it conforms to the structure of the document type defined by the DTD. DTDs are almost always written with specific processing or results in mind but can easily be re-purposed. Since SGML markup is application independent, it means that documents that conform to a particular DTD can be re-used in a variety of different ways. Knowing that a document is structured in a specific way makes subsequent reuse of the document easier.

There are three different functional parts of an SGML document. The first specifies the character set of the document; the second part names the document type and, thus, the specific tags that can be used in the document. The third part of an SGML document is the actual text or content, marked with SGML tags.

For example, a "poem" could be defined as a document type. The DTD for "poem" could define lines and stanzas (tags: <line> and <stanza>) as the required elements. Optional elements could include <couplets>, <octaves>, <sestets>, <footnotes>, and <author>; these elements may be present in a document defined as a poem, but need not be. The purpose of the DTD and SGML coding might be to print all the tagged poems with octaves in bold and sestets in italics, using a translation program of some sort. The might be a need later to print the same tagged poems with only octaves in italics; it would not be necessary to re-tag each poem, but only to alter the translation program that processed the tagged texts. Indeed, the possible uses of the tagged poems is virtually limitless since almost any processing instructions can be applied. Different sorts of processing instructions can be associated with the same parts of the file. For example, a program for textual analysis could ignore footnotes in a tagged poem that a program for printing might collect for printing at the end of each poem. The same print program might extract authors' names from the poems to print at the top of each poem; the textual analysis program could use the authors' names to create a searchable database. The combination of descriptive markup and document type definitions allow SGML-encoded documents to be processed by many different pieces of software with many different results in mind. Because SGML is non-proprietary (not owned by a single computer hardware or software manufacturer) and is an international standard, data remains independent of any particular hardware or software configuration making SGML, and SGML-conformant applications extremely flexible.

SGML has many features that defied convenient description with the popular formal automata theory and the contemporary parser technology of the 1980s and the 1990s. The standard warns in Annex H:

The SGML model group notation was deliberately designed to resemble the regular expression notation of automata theory, because automata theory provides a theoretical foundation for some aspects of the notion of conformance to a content model. No assumption should be made about the general applicability of automata to content models.

A report on an early implementation of a parser for basic SGML, the Amsterdam SGML Parser, note the DTD-grammar in SGML must conform to a notion of unambiguity which closely resembles the LL(1) conditions and specifies various differences.

There appears to be no definitive classification of full SGML against a known class of formal grammar. Plausible classes may include tree-adjoining grammars and adaptive grammars.

XML is described as being generally parsable like a two-level grammar for non-validated XML and a Conway-style pipeline of coroutines (lexer, parser, validator) for valid XML. The SGML productions in the ISO standard are reported to be LL(3) or LL(4).[11] XML-class subsets are reported to be expressible using a W-grammar. According to one paper, and probably considered at information set or parse tree level rather than a character or delimiter level:

The class of documents that conform to a given SGML document grammar forms an LL(1) language. ... The SGML document grammars by themselves are, however, not LL(1) grammars.

The SGML standard does not define SGML with formal data structures, such as parse trees; however, an SGML document is constructed of a rooted directed acyclic graph (RDAG) of physical storage units known as "entities", which is parsed into a RDAG of structural units known as "elements". The physical graph is loosely characterized as an entity tree, but entities might appear multiple times. Moreover, the structure graph is also loosely characterized as an element tree, but the ID/IDREF markup allows arbitrary arcs.

The results of parsing can also be understood as a data tree in different notations; where the document is the root node, and entities in other notations (text, graphics) are child nodes. SGML provides apparatus for linking to and annotating external non-SGML entities.

The SGML standard describes it in terms of maps and recognition modes (s9.6.1). Each entity, and each element, can have an associated notation or declared content type, which determines the kinds of references and tags which will be recognized in that entity and element. Also, each element can have an associated delimiter map (and short reference map), which determines which characters are treated as delimiters in context. The SGML standard characterizes parsing as a state machine switching between recognition modes. During parsing, there is a stack of maps that configure the scanner, while the tokenizer relates to the recognition modes.

Parsing involves traversing the dynamically-retrieved entity graph, finding/implying tags and the element structure, and validating those tags against the grammar. An unusual aspect of SGML is that the grammar (DTD) is used both passively – to recognize lexical structures, and actively – to generate missing structures and tags that the DTD has declared optional. End- and start- tags can be omitted, because they can be inferred. Loosely, a series of tags can be omitted only if there is a single, possible path in the grammar to imply them. It was this active use of grammars that made concrete SGML parsing difficult to formally characterize.

SGML uses the term validation for both recognition and generation. XML does not use the grammar (DTD) to change delimiter maps or to inform the parse modes, and does not allow tag omission; consequently, XML validation of elements is not active in the sense that SGML validation is active. SGML without a DTD (e.g. simple XML), is a grammar or a language; SGML with a DTD is a metalanguage. SGML with an SGML declaration is, perhaps, a meta-metalanguage, since it is a metalanguage whose declaration mechanism is a metalanguage.

SGML has an abstract syntax implemented by many possible concrete syntaxes; however, this is not the same usage as in an abstract syntax tree and as in a concrete syntax tree. In the SGML usage, a concrete syntax is a set of specific delimiters, while the abstract syntax is the set of names for the delimiters. The XML Infoset corresponds more to the programming language notion of abstract syntax introduced by John McCarthy.

2.5.1. SGML, Markup and the Online Library System

What then is the relationship of SGML to an online library system? Three projects and initiatives that are currently underway can serve as examples of the usefulness of markup to library information retrieval and selection. These three projects all make use of SGML in providing structure and access to bibliographical information.

2.5.2. The Text Encoding Initiative(*http://www.uic.edu/orgs/tei/*)

The Text Encoding Initiative (TEI) is an international, cooperative project to develop guidelines for the preparation and interchange of electronic texts for scholarly research. TEI prepared the *Guidelines for Text Encoding and Interchange*

(Sperberg-McQueen, *http://etext.virginia.edu/TEI.html*) to develop

"A common encoding scheme for complex textual structures in order to reduce the diversity of existing encoding practices, simplifies processing by machine, and encourages the sharing of electronic texts." (Sperberg- McQueen, preface).

The TEI header, a mandatory part of TEI-conformant texts, has four major parts: a file description, which contains a full bibliographical description of the computer file itself and includes information about the source or sources from which the electronic text was derived; an encoding description, which describes the relationship between an electronic text and its source or sources. It allows for detailed description of whether (or how) the text was normalized during transcription, how the encoder resolved ambiguities in the source, and the like; a text profile containing classificatory and contextual information about the text, such as its subject matter, the situation in which it was produced, the individuals described by or participating in producing it, and so forth; and a revision history, which allows the encoder to provide a history of changes made during the development of the electronic text (Sperberg-McQueen, 5.1.1). The guidelines for the TEI header include discussion of the header's relationship to the MARC record. The guidelines state that TEI's goal in creating the header is "to ensure that the information required for a catalogue record be retrievable from the TEI file header, and moreover that the mapping from the one to the other be as simple and straightforward as possible."

The most important difference between the MARC record and the TEI header is the function of each. Despite the efforts and claims of some members of the library community, the MARC record remains fundamentally an electronic version of the catalogue card, with the limitations of its model. The primary function of the MARC record when it was first designed in the mid-1960s was to allow for the electronic distribution of cataloguing records in support of card production ... The catalogue card is a unitary record for a physical object containing complex bibliographic data of varying sorts. The catalogue card points to the physical object. The TEI header provides full bibliographic information (as would a card), as well as documentary non-bibliographic information that supports the analysis, either by humans or machines, of the electronic text documented by header. Most of this analytical information, which is found in profile description, encoding description, and revision history, has little direct provision for it in the MARC record, and if retained must be recorded as unstructured notes (5XX) fields. Notes fields usually do not have the structure to support machine retrieval and analysis, while properly formatted profile, encoding, and revision descriptions lend themselves to retrieval, can support machine processing (including analysis), and point directly to the electronic text attached to the header. Moreover, the electronic text points back to the relevant elements in the header.

2.5.3. Finding Aids For Archival Collections (*http://sunsite.berkeley.edu/FindingAids/*)

The Finding Aids for Archival Collections is a collaborative project to develop an encoding standard for archive, museum, and library finding aids. "Finding aids are documents used to describe, control, and provide access to collections of related materials. In the hierarchical structure of collection-level information access and navigation, finding aids reside between bibliographic records and the primary source materials. Bibliographic records lead to finding aids, and finding aids lead to primary source materials." (Finding Aids for Archival Collections). The goals of the project are two-fold. First, to create a prototype encoding standard for finding aids in the form of an SGML DTD. Second, to build a prototype database of finding aids. The database is to serve two purposes.

First, it provides the encoding standard developers with

computer application experience with which to refine and inform the development process. Second, it provides a means for end users to evaluate the utility and desirability of encoded finding aids, which, in turn, enables them to provide new ideas and suggestions to the encoding standard developers. (Finding Aids for Archival Collections)

SGML was chosen over MARC for encoding the records because of MARC's limited accommodation of hierarchically structured information. Since finding aids are hierarchically structured documents, the flat structure of MARC makes it unsatisfactory. As archivists are painfully aware, MARC was primarily designed to capture description and access information applying to a discrete bibliographic item. Describing and providing access to complex collections through descending levels of analysis quickly overburdens the MARC structure. At most, a second level of analysis can be accommodated, but the kind of information so supplied is limited. One possible way around this problem is to employ multiple, hierarchically interrelated and interlinked records at varying levels of analysis: collection-level, subunit, and item. The use of multiple records, though, introduces extremely difficult inter- and intra-system control problems that have never been adequately addressed in the format or by MARC based software developers. (Pitti, section "MARC vs. SGML")

2.5.4. Columbia University Digital Image Access Project (DIAP) (*http://www.cc.columbia.edu/cu/libraries/indiv/avery/diap.html*

The cooperative Research Libraries Group initiative on access to digital images has prompted the Columbia University Libraries to suggest a new model for housing and access to bibliographic and analytical data on digital images. Columbia's DIAP team suggests that data could readily be "housed" in an SGML-encoded bibliographic (metadata) record that encapsulates both summary bibliographic information along with detailed hierarchical and version-related data, when such data is appropriate and considered useful to record. The record would also include links to the actual digital items, to other related bibliographic records or, in fact, to diverse, related digital objects (such as external electronic publications, databases, numeric files, etc.) The working designation SGML Catalog Record (SCR) is proposed for this new type of record. The SCR would, by flexibly incorporating data-element "clusters," allow a more narrative approach to the recording and presentation of complex bibliographic information than is practical in the current AACR2/USMARC model, which requires the fragmentation of hierarchically-related components and version information into separate, discrete records. That the current USMARC model serves libraries and users poorly—most notably in the cataloging of microfilm reproductions of printed texts and with complex serial publications—has been widely discussed. Attempts to rectify the situation have been unsuccessful, in large part because of the intrinsically flat structure of USMARC and the automated library systems that have been designed around it.

The Columbia proposal also suggests that libraries "would for the present, and perhaps indefinitely," continue to create summary MARC records—with pointers to the SCRs—in local online systems and national utilities.

2.6. HTML5

Hypertext markup language is used to aid in the

publication of web pages by providing a structure that defines elements like tables, forms, lists and headings, and identifies where different portions of our content begin and end. It can be used to embed other file formats like videos, audio files, documents like PDFs and spreadsheets, among others. HTML is the most relied upon language in the creation of web sites. In this text we will focus on HTML5. While it is technically still in draft form, many proposed elements are already supported by the newer versions of most of the popular browsers.

2.6.1. History

In the beginning, back to the first days of the Internet and ARPA, the primary purpose of creating a page was to share research and information. HTML tags were only meant to provide layout and formatting of a page. As such, early implementations of HTML were somewhat limited as there was little demand for features beyond the basics. Headings, bullets, tables, and color were about all developers had to utilize. As sites were created for other more commercial uses, developers found creative ways of using these tools to get their pages looking more like magazines, advertisements, and what they had drawn on paper. Having been one of those developers, I recall the days of just-get-it-looking-right techniques, splicing page-sized images into tables so graphics were (usually) where we wanted them, nesting tables within tables to create complex layouts, and other methods that violate today's best practices.

2.6.2. Current State

While not formally finalized, many browsers are already supporting a number of features proposed in drafts of HTML5, including things like canvas and media support that greatly improve the browser's ability to process and display complex materials without requiring extensive coding and extensions. In the past, sites that used video and audio players had to integrate support for many players, and would have to include the libraries and formatted files for those systems in their sites. By providing a solution to using these media forms within HTML5, we can improve on the user experience and reduce the efforts necessary to provide them.

While these new features do reduce the amount of programming required to implement higher level elements, and include interactive elements that exceed document markup activities, HTML5 is still considered a markup language.

In these languages, we use tags to ascribe additional meaning to our text, which provide instruction to the browser as to how to display the text on the screen, but are not necessarily displayed to the user. In HTML and XHTML these tags are fixed, or predefined, meaning the names that can be used in the tags are limited to what browsers are able to recognize. In XML, tags are defined by the person creating the content as they are typically used in conjunction with data sources and provide information.

2.6.3. W3C Standards

The *World Wide Web Consortium*, or W3C, is an international community that supports web development through the creation of open standards that provide the best user experience possible for the widest audience of users. This group of professionals and experts come together to determine how CSS and HTML should operate, what tags should be included as features, and more. The W3C is also your best reference point in determining the accessibility of your site through the use of tools that analyze your code for W3C compliance. These tools confirm if you have fully implemented elements in your code, like providing alternate text descriptions of images in the event that the image cannot load, or the user is visually impaired.

In addition to the creation of accessibility standards, among many others, the W3C also provides tutorials and examples and is likely the most exhaustive reference you will find.

2.6.4. Programming Languages in Library and Information Science

Different programming languages address different kinds of problems. To understand which are most suitable for library and information science (LIS), first define the kinds of programming problems these areas present.

Library and information science (LIS) programming divides into two classes: problems that are similar to those of business and government, and those that are unique to library and information science. The former consist of front office applications, such as word processing, spread sheets and desktop computing, and back office applications, comprising data processing functions like accounts payable and receivable, payroll and other business operations. Together they comprise information technology (IT). For IT applications, Library and information science (LIS) employs the same programming languages as other organizations. Their goals are the same.

Library and information science (LIS) also presents unique requirements. These derive from the need for text processing – the ability to analyze, process and reformat text. Examples include products created by computer text manipulation, such as concordances, indexes, bibliographies and citation maps. Information retrieval (IR) is another area. The goal is to rapidly retrieve relevant information by applying Boolean logic to keywords and searching databases optimized for textual storage and retrieval. A third area is linguistic research and natural language processing. Textual analysis answers all manner of research questions. The classic is: Who was Shakespeare and were all his works written by one person? A more recent example attempted to predict the effectiveness of the 2004 presidential candidates by analyzing how they expressed concepts in their speeches.

These problems all require text processing. Text consists of words (and structural syntax) combined into larger units like sentences, paragraphs and documents. A single sequence of letters is a *character string* or *string*. String manipulation includes several operations. Strings must be *parsed* or scanned for specific sub strings and split into their constituent sub strings. Pattern matching refers to how strings are inspected and their contents analyzed. Bifurcation splits strings into components. Concatenation joins two or more strings into one.

Languages implement string processing through operators that manipulate strings within expressions. Functions or object methods perform additional string operations. External or callable libraries contain additional functions or object methods.

Whether a programming language is suitable for Library and information science (LIS) depends on how well that language processes text. A suitable language means smaller, simpler programs. Fewer errors occur. Programs are easier to enhance and maintain. An unsuitable language means more code, more effort and greater likelihood of error. Programs are difficult to enhance and maintain.

2.6.5. Beginnings

Early programmers worked in native computer code or machine language. This was tedious, error prone and labor intensive. The first higher level languages leveraged computer power to address the problem. Each reflected a different understanding of how to conceptualize programming problems, a different programming paradigm. FORTRAN views problems through the prism of numeric formulas and calculations. COBOL processes records and thereby forms the basis for library data processing. LISP resolves problems by manipulating lists.

The first language based on a string processing paradigm was COMIT. Defects marked it as an early effort. SNOBOL (StriNg Oriented SymBOlic Language) was the first viable string processing language. It reached its final form by 1969 as SNOBOL4.

SNOBOL features exceptionally powerful pattern matching, string substitution and replacement. Problems that might require hundreds of lines of code in unsuitable languages (say, COBOL or Pascal) can be resolved in small, easily understood SNOBOL programs.

These advantages won SNOBOL its role as the primary language for specialized text analysis and research during the 1970s and 1980s. But SNOBOL remained outside of mainstream computing. The language is resource intensive, runs only on certain computers and offers meager facilities outside of string processing. Its input/output model, mathematical abilities and control constructs are limited.

In contrast to SNOBOL's specialization, PL/I was the first general purpose programming language to offer strong string manipulation capabilities. It attained mainstream popularity by combining the formulaic abilities of FORTRAN with the record processing features of COBOL and integrating string processing. PL/I first proved the efficacy of the text processing paradigm to many in computing.

Through the 1970s and 1980s, PL/I was the primary text processing language for librarians and information scientists, while SNOBOL held sway among those in specialized text analysis and university research.

2.6.6. HTML5 Features

HTML5 provides new features that include

- Canvas – 2D/3D Graphics
- Audio & Video
- Location based Services

- Working Offline
- Web Workers
- Drag & Drop
- New Input Types
- New Elements
- Form Elements

New Elements in HTML5 : In HTML 4.01 several elements are outdated, never used, or not used the way they were pre planned. All these elements are abolished or re-written in HTML5.

The elements which are deprecated in HTML5 are as follows:

- <acronym>
- <applet>
- <basefont>
- <big>
- <center>
- <dir>
- <font>
- <frame>
- <frameset>
- <isindex>
- <noframes>
- <s>
- <strike>
- <tt>
- <u>

To better serve today's web requirements, HTML5 has also introduced new elements for drawing graphics, displaying media content, for better page structure and better form handling, and several new APIs for drag and drop, for finding your geological location, for storing local data, and more.

2.7. EXTENSIBLE MARKUP LANGUAGE (XML)

The Extensible Markup Language (XML), as specified in the World Wide Web Consortium's (W3C) Recommendation approved on February 10, 1998, is a subset of the Standard Generalized Markup Language (SGML) defined in ISO standard 8879:1986 that is designed to make it easy to interchange structured documents over the Internet. XML files always clearly mark where the start and end of each of the logical parts (called *elements*) of an interchanged document occurs. XML restricts the use of SGML constructs to ensure that fallback options are available when access to certain components of the document is not currently possible over the Internet. It also defines how Internet Uniform Resource Locators can be used to identify component parts of XML data streams.

By defining the role of each element of text in a formal model, known as a Document Type Definition (DTD), users of XML can check that each component of a document occurs in a valid place within the interchanged data stream. An XML DTD allows computers to check, for example, that users do not accidentally enter a third level heading without first having entered a second level heading, something that cannot be checked using the Hypertext Markup Language (HTML) previously used to code documents that form part of the World Wide Web (WWW) of documents accessible through the Internet.

The last decade has seen the rapid expansion of the eXtensible Markup Language in many application ûelds. Born as the successor of SGML, XML soon became the natural way of representing data with loose structure; furthermore, its great ûexibility made it a universal data representation format, and allowed the use of XML as a convenient medium for exchanging data between different applications. Finally, XML also acquired an important role in data exchange and data integration systems.

To support the diffusion of XML, several tools for transforming, querying, manipulating, and modeling XML data have been deûned. In particular, the World Wide Web Consortium (W3C) introduced XQuery [XQub] as the standard query language for XML data. Since its introduction, XQuery has attracted a big deal of attention, from both industrial and academic worlds. The research community has been involved in many research directions such as complexity and expressivity analysis of XQuery fragments, techniques to optimize query evaluation, security, static analysis, and data integration.

However, unlike SGML, XML does not require the presence of a DTD. If no DTD is available, either because all or part of it is not accessible over the Internet or because the user failed to create it, an XML system can assign a default definition for undeclared components of the markup. XML allows users to

- bring multiple files together to form compound documents
- identify where illustrations are to be incorporated into text files, and the format used to encode each illustration
- provide processing control information to supporting programs, such as document validators and browsers
- add editorial comments to a file.
- It is important to note, however, that XML is not
- a predefined set of tags, of the type defined for HTML, that can be used to markup documents
- a standardized template for producing particular types of documents.

XML was not designed to be a standardized way of

coding text; in fact, it is impossible to devise a single coding scheme that would suit all languages and all applications. Instead XML is formal language that can be used to pass information about the component parts of a document to another computer system. XML is flexible enough to be able to describe any logical text structure, whether it be a form, memo, letter, report, book, encyclopedia, dictionary or database.

2.7.1. The Components of XML

XML is based on the concept of *documents* composed of a series of *entities*. (People familiar with modern programming techniques will probably be more comfortable using the word *object*, which is synonymous in this case.) Each entity can contain one or more logical *elements*. Each of these elements can have certain *attributes* (properties) that describe the way in which it is to be processed. XML provides a formal syntax for describing the relationships between the entities, elements and attributes that make up an XML document, which can be used to tell the computer how it can recognize the component parts of each document.

XML differs from other markup languages in that it does not simply indicate where a change of appearance occurs or where a new element starts. XML sets out to clearly identify the boundaries of every part of a document, whether it be a new chapter, a piece of boilerplate text or a reference to another publication.

To allow the computer to check the structure of a document users must provide it with a document type definition that declares each of the permitted entities, elements and attributes and the relationships among them.

2.7.2. The Use of XML

To use a set of *markup tags* that has been defined by a trade association or similar body, users need to know how the markup tags are delimited from normal text and in which order the various elements should be used. Systems that understand XML can provide users with lists of the elements that are valid at each point in the document and will automatically add the required delimiters to the name to produce a markup tag. Where the data capture system does not understand XML, users can enter the XML tags manually for later validation. Elements and their attributes are entered between matched pairs of angle brackets (<...>) while entity references start with an ampersand and end with a semicolon (&...;).

Because XML tag sets are based on the logical structure of the document, they are somewhat easier to understand and remember than physically based markup schemes of the type typically provided by word processors. An XML memo might be coded as follows:

```
<memo>
<to>All staff</to>
<from>Martin Bryan</from>
<date>5th November</date>
<subject>Cats and Dogs</subject>
<text>Please remember to keep all cats and dogs indoors
tonight.</text>
</memo>
```

This form is ideal for a computer to follow and, therefore, to process. The start and end of each logical element of the file has been clearly identified by entry of a start tag (e.g., **<to>**) and an end tag (e.g., **</to>**).

Notice that at this point nothing has been said about the format of the final document. From the neutral format provided by XML, users can either choose to display the memo on a screen, whose size can be varied to suit user preferences, to print the text onto a pre printed form or to generate a completely new form, positioning each element of the document where needed.

2.7.3. Storage and Indexing

Lore uses a simple storage manager that parses XML into the basic units of elements, attributes, and text strings, and stores them using a straightforward depth-first clustering heuristic. We can build a wide variety of indexes on Lore databases. The types of indexes we support were designed for Lore's original data model, OEM, but with minor changes the indexes also work for XML. There are several further avenues to pursue in storage and indexing:

- Different clustering schemes for storing XML data, preferably customizable for different databases and applications.
- New index types designed specifically for XML data, taking into account element ordering, new kinds of comparison operations, and a few other subtle differences between XML and our original data model.
- More radically, we plan to explore using XML documents themselves as a storage medium in Lore, augmented with auxiliary structures such as: (1) an indexing scheme for quickly finding certain elements, attributes, and more complex structural patterns in the document; and/or (2) a data store containing some of the XML data parsed to some level (and possibly created "lazily", i.e., on an as-needed basis), with a mapping maintained between the database and documents.
- Depending on how applications tend to encode their data in XML, we may find that we can take data that is primarily encoded as tree structures and convert it to a more graph-structured representation, e.g., by merging identical text values or entire subelements, then inserting appropriate IDREFs. It will be interesting to see whether any significant compression is achieved, but more importantly to observe the effect on query processing and even query semantics.

- Another opportunity for compressing XML data is to exploit regularity in the structure, in the extreme case storing the XML data essentially as relations.

2.8. Summary

So we can say that *all the scripting languages are programming languages but all the programming languages are not scripting languages.* C cannot be called a scripting language, it is just a programming language but we can call JavaScript or Php programming or scripting languages. Also, there is no need to compile scripting languages it only needs to be interpreted. Scripting languages are generally slower than programming languages because compiled programs are first converted into machine code. On the other hand, markup languages are just used to define the structure of data which doesn't require any logic or algorithm.

2.9. REVIEW QUESTION

1. Define Markup Languages?
2. List HTML5 FEATURES?
3. Uses of XML?

Unit 3

OBJECTIVES

- To learn tool and technique of Adobe PDF
- To provide access to information at a faster rate
- To create a document by selecting one of the numerous presets available in Photoshop

3.1. INTRODUCTION

Portable document format (PDF) is one of the most popular file formats for displaying and printing documents. When this format was released by Adobe in 1993, it shared many of the same concepts and components of PostScript. But where PostScript was designed primarily to provide device independent consistency in print output, PDF was focused on maintaining the visual appearance of a document onscreen, independent of the operating system displaying it. Over the years, PDF has expanded to more specific-use specifications for engineering, archiving, health care, universal access, and printing. A series of recent studies has indicated that a mixed signal device analog to digital converters used for the processing of information and play a vital role in wireless sensors, Digital signal processing, Biomedical devices, in communication, IOT and various other applications. Across this broad use they give the significance in designing. The paper represents the various parameters like speed, area occupied, power consumption, sampling Rate, precision, Signal to noise ratio, Signal to noise distortion ratio, resolution, linearity and conversion time with respect to its different types and broad application in the real world. It defines errors due to non - linearity of signals as Differential nonlinearity, Integral nonlinearity, gain error, quantization error, aliasing and offset error. It also gives the comparative study about ADCs.

3.2. PAGE DESCRIPTION LANGUAGES (PCL)

A page description language is a programming language used to describe the structure and appearance of a document page, in a device (printer) independent way. A document description language is a language which not only specifies structure and appearance of a page, but also the structure of a document, the global document composing environment, and relationships between pages, combining pages of one document within another document, etc. The printing environment specification subset of a language, is used to specify printing options like one sided, and two sided printing, paper-shift during the printing of a page, tray used to feed in paper to print the entire document or on a page basis, etc.

There are two objectives in presenting this paper. First, to present the concepts of page and document description, as well as printing environment specification languages, and second to describe experience gained in two implementations related to Interpress, a XEROX developed document description language incorporating a printing environment specification subset.In digital printing, a page description language (PDL) is a computer language that describes the appearance of a printed page in a higher level than an actual output bitmap (or generally raster graphics). An overlapping term is printer control language, which includes Hewlett-Packard's Printer Command Language (PCL). PostScript is one of the most noted page description languages. The markup language adaptation of the PDL is the page description markup language.

Page description languages are text (human-readable) or binary data streams, usually intermixed with text or graphics to be printed. They are distinct from graphics application programming interfaces (APIs) such as GDI and OpenGL that can be called by software to generate graphical output. Many page description languages (PDL) exist today; however, Printer Command Language (PCL) and PostScript are the most common and widely adopted. Each has its strengths, weaknesses, and jobs for which it is best suited. It is important to understand these differences and choose the method best suited to your particular printing requirements.

PCL is a page description language developed by Hewlett-Packard (HP) and was originally used on HP impact and inkjet printers. PCL 3 was the first version to be used with a laser printer, the HP LaserJet, released in 1984, around the same time PostScript was introduced. The goal of PCL was to have an efficient printer control language that could be implemented consistently across HP's printer line. Simple commands and functionality would not require expensive print controllers, making it very attractive for utility-level printing. Many other printer manufacturers implemented PCL for this reason. Commands are embedded at the beginning of the print job and set the parameters for the printer to use for the job. These commands remain set until a new value is assigned for the command or the printer is reset. If the printer does not support a specific command, it ignores it.

When colour laser printing became available, PCL 5c was developed with similar goals. New commands were added to the existing command set, as was the case with all the predecessors, to add support for colour printing. This ensured backwards compatibility while minimizing development. When it came to colour, HP's goal was to have colour on the printed page look the same as what was displayed on screen. There were many challenges to achieving this, so print quality adjustments were included to give users the ability to fine-tune the output. With the emergence and widespread adoption of the sRGB standard to define and describe colour on a display, the PCL colour command set could be simplified by adopting this standard for colour printing. Thus, HP's goal could be achieved without the complexity and overhead of a full colour management system. Operating systems and applications, for the most part, have standardized how they display colour in sRGB, so this approach is the simplest way to achieve acceptable colour between display and print. PCL is most appropriate for general office use where a simple, low-cost print device that produces good quality colour is expected. It is not suitable, however, for a colour critical or print production environment where precision and full colour management is required.

3.2.1. PostScript

PostScript is a page description and programming language developed by Adobe that describes text, graphics, and images, and their placement on a page, independent of the intended output destination. The code created is in plain text that can be written and examined with a basic text editor. The output itself can either be to a printer, display, or other device possessing a PostScript interpreter, making it a device independent language. The interpreter processes the PostScript instructions to create a raster image the device can render. The interpreter is often referred to as a RIP or raster image processor for this reason. It is possible to write valid PostScript code from scratch, but it is impractical as page composition applications can either generate the PostScript code directly or can utilize a print driver, which can convert the page to the PostScript language.

Since PostScript is a general-purpose programming language, it includes many elements that you wouldn't associate specifically with printing such as data types (numbers, arrays, and strings) and control primitives (conditionals, loops, and procedures). It also has an interesting feature called dictionary, which stores information in a table consisting of a collection of key and value pairs. The values can be entered into the dictionary while the keys are used to reference the information needed. These features made possible documents that acted like an application which could generate pages dynamically from data directly on the printer itself. These printer-based applications were stored temporarily in memory or permanently in the printer's hard drive, and triggered by a command in the print stream. These capabilities made variable data printing possible using PostScript and are still being used today for that purpose.

The first printer to use PostScript was the Apple LaserWriter in 1985. The same day that Apple announced the LaserWriter, Aldus Corporation announced PageMaker, a page layout application developed to take advantage of the Apple Macintosh computer's GUI (graphical user interface) and the PostScript PDL. This series of events is considered by many as the genesis of the desktop publishing revolution. In fact, the term *desktop publishing* is attributed to the founder of Aldus Corporation.

3.2.2. Portable document format (PDF)

Portable document format (PDF) is one of the most popular file formats for displaying and printing documents. When this format was released by Adobe in 1993, it shared many of the same concepts and components of PostScript. But where PostScript was designed primarily to provide device independent consistency in print output, PDF was focused on maintaining the visual appearance of a document onscreen, independent of the operating system displaying it. Over the years, PDF has expanded to more specific-use specifications for engineering, archiving, health care, universal access, and printing.

PDF/X is a branch of PDF and an ISO standard that deals specifically with print. It was developed by the Committee for Graphic Arts Technologies Standards (CGATS). Table 6.5 shows the evolution of the standard.

The below Table Evolution of PDFData source: Adobe Systems Inc, 2008, p. 4

Preset	*Compatibility*	*Settings*	*Usage*
PDF/X-1a: 2001 PDF/X-1a: 2003	Acrobat 4/PDF 1.3 Acrobat 5/PDF 1.4	• Convert RGB colour to CMYK (spot colors allowed) • Transparency flattened	PDF/X-1a ensures that the files are ready for print production—fonts are embedded, colours must be CMYK or spot, layers and transparency are flattened. Note

			that there is no minimum resolution required for PDF/X.
PDF/X-3: 2002	Acrobat 4/PDF 1.3	• Leave RGB and CIELab color unchanged (profiles allowed) • Transparency flattened	PDF/X-3 has all the benefits of PDF/X-1a plus it allows colour-managed workflows.
PDF/X-3: 2003 PDF/X-4: 2008	Acrobat 5/PDF 1.4 Acrobat 7/PDF 1.6	• Leave RGB and CIELab colour unchanged (profiles allowed) • Live (unflattened) transparency • Layers allowed	Has all the benefits of PDF/X-3 plus it allows live (unflattened) transparency and layers for versioning. Print workflows based on the Adobe PDF Print Engine will be able to process PDF/X-4 jobs natively, without flattening artwork or converting to PostScript.
PDF/X-4p: 2008	Acrobat 7/PDF 1.6		Use PDF/X-4p when a required ICC profile is unambiguously identified and supplied separately.

Submitting documents for print using one of these standards is highly recommended as it eliminates many of the causes of print issues and is a more reliable method for graphics file exchange.

3.2.3. Digital Front End (DFE)

Digital front end (DFE) describes the combination of hardware and software that drives and manages a print device. Hardware is often custom built for this specific purpose and may have proprietary video interfaces that connect directly to the print engine. An operating system serves as the base for the software components of the DFE and is often Microsoft Windows based or a Linux or Unix variant. Although the Windows running on a DFE is much the same as its desktop counterpart, Linux- and Unix-based systems are often custom distributions that are compiled specifically for the DFE.

One of the key components of a DFE is the raster image processor (RIP). The RIP refers to the software component that interprets the PDL and performs the function of rendering or rasterizing the complete instructions into an image or raster the print engine will reproduce. The term RIP is often used interchangeably with DFE. This may have been accurate in the past when a DFE really only performed the ripping function and little else. Modern DFEs, however, do much more. In fact, a DFE may contain multiple RIPs, and within those RIPs they can utilize the multi-threading and processing power of modern computer hardware and operating systems to process many pages or channels simultaneously. PostScript has been the defacto PDL in digital printing for many years but with the development of the PDF/X print standards and the subsequent release of the Adobe PDF Print Engine (APPE), a native PDF RIP, many DFEs now include both PostScript and APPE as their available RIP engines.

ICC-based colour management workflow may be part of the RIP process or can be an independent component of the DFE. Different elements within a print file get processed through their respective channels in the colour management system. Common channels include CMYK, RGB, black, and named colours. The idea is to convert all colour elements into the colour gamut of the print engine's colorants/paper combination. The conversion process can be complicated, but the basic concept is device dependent source colour spaces (CMYK, RGB, etc.) are converted to a device independent colour space, referred to the profile conversion space (PSC), then from the PSC to the output gamut defined in the output ICC profile. The idea is to take the source 'recipe' and define the visual appearance of it first. That is why it needs to convert to device independent colour space, which defines the visual appearance of colour. Once the visual appearance is defined, the 'recipe' for the specific output can be calculated.

Systems that support named or spot colour rendering follow a similar process. The named colour is located in a look up table. The name must match perfectly, including punctuation, spaces, and case. Each named colour is defined in a device independent colour space, typically Lab. There is no calculation in this step. The last step is the same; Lab values are then converted via the output profile.

There is one more calculation applied before passing the information through to the printer. Electro photography is affected by rapid changes in humidity and temperature. The electro photographic process relies on components that do become less effective over time and use. These factors all affect the color output. Calibration should be performed on a regular basis to compensate for these variables. Calibration is a process of creating a correction curve to maintain consistent and repeatable print output. This correction curve is applied right after the conversion to output profile, ensuring output is consistent with what was defined in the output profile itself.

In order to maintain all these aspects of the DFE, an intuitive and user-friendly interface is critical. The user interface includes many components. Here is where you would configure the DFE, find the status of the print device and consumables, view and process jobs and job queues, and examine and export job histories and logs. Many WYSIWYG tools are accessed via the user interface, such as those for workflow, imposition, complex job composition, paper libraries, spot color refinement, the launching of external tools, and even interfaces into other systems such as web2print. DFEs are becoming more powerful and perform more than just the traditional RIP functions. As the digital print industry continues to evolve, DFEs will be called on to perform more duties and functions. User interfaces will need to evolve as well to maintain usability and stay intuitive.

Page Description Language (PDL) software is the brains behind devices that print, view or exchange files. PDF, PostScript, PCL, OpenXPS, and PPML are popular Page Description Languages that describe the content and layout of a document, typically to an imaging device or a mobile application. Since the PDL is responsible for what goes on the page, it's critical for your PDL implementation to be accurate, robust and conform to the PDL specification.

There are endless combinations of PDL operators and attributes your product needs to correctly render. In addition, hundreds of different applications and apps produce documents. Each may exercise a different mix of PDL features to describe the original content. To be sure your implementation is successful; you must test these capabilities in depth and in a systematic manner.

That's where we come in. Quality Logic has been developing PDL test tools for over three decades. We know PDL specifications and testing issues from the inside out. The test tools we've developed are industry standards used by leading printer, application, and technology vendors globally. We can also use our full suite of tools to test your printer or MFP for you.

3.3. PAGE DESCRIPTION LANGUAGE TEST TOOLS TO COVER ALL THE BASES

Quality Logic approaches PDL testing by basing test cases entirely on the capabilities of the PDL standard itself – not just what popular applications or drivers are generating currently. Typical documents use much less than what the PDL standard supports.

3.3.1. Functional Test Suites (FTSs)

FTSs test the basic functionality of each command or operator in a PDL, quickly assessing baseline conformance to the language specification. They are a cost-effective and efficient way to assure the basic functionality of your PDL and are designed to the following criteria:

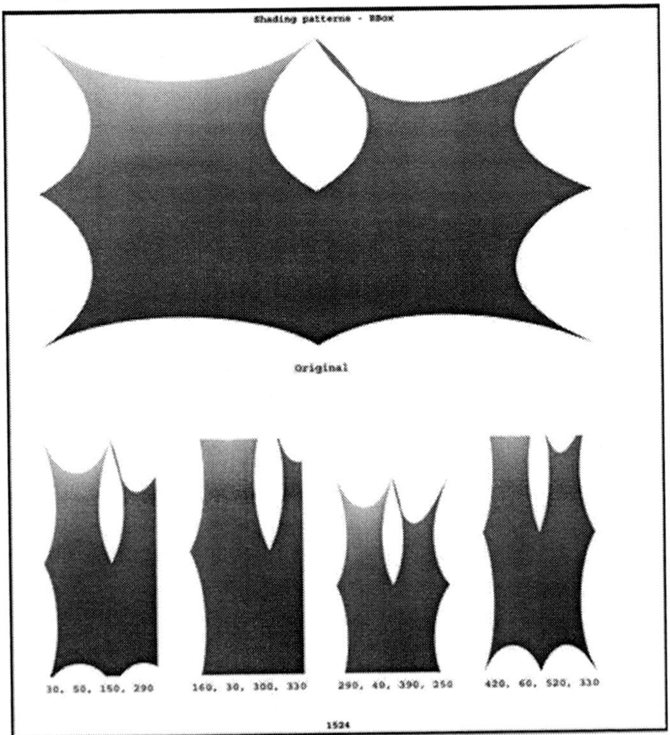

- Must run unattended in 24 hours or less – ideal for regression test runs
- Multiple test cases per page to minimize paper consumption
- Cover the breadth of the PDL standard by exercising each key PDL operator
- All test cases are developed to control the PDL operators within each test file
- Each test case has clearly documented test intent and can be debugged quickly

3.3.2. Comprehensive Evaluation Tests (CETs)

CETs go beyond the FTS. They include a deeper level of tests covering all commands and combinations allowed in the PDL standard, as well as illegal sequences. CETs provide the most challenging test scenarios that your implementation will encounter. CETs include the following types of tests for all major PDLs:

Standard Tests to cover common objectives for a wide variety of commands or operators using various combinations and data types

Influence Tests for the interactive influence of commands or operators (graphics states, opacity, transform, etc.)

Special Tests covering definitive statements in the language specification outside the scope of Standard or Influence Tests

Error Tests of conditions found when consuming a file, including out-of-range parameters and illegal command sequences

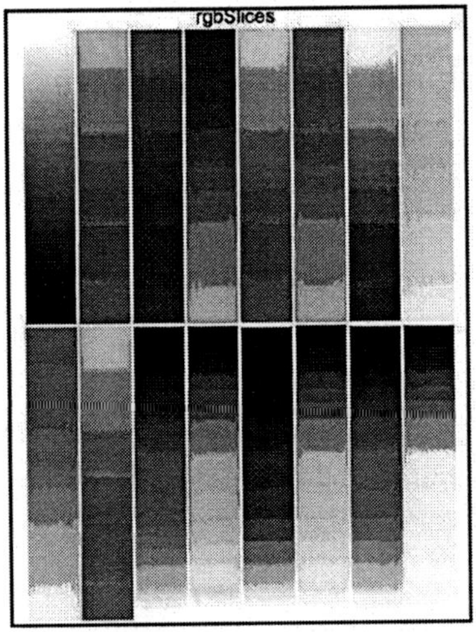

3.3.3. Application Test Suites (ATSs)

Use ATSs to test your printer, MFP, or software product for compatibility with leading applications, drivers, and content creators. They are comprehensive collections of test pages developed using all of the most popular applications. We designed ATS test files to help you ensure compatibility in the real world with the applications your customers use with your product. ATSs help you:

Improve Time-To-Market – ATS files are provided in captured binary format, so you don't have to purchase dozens of applications and develop test pages.

Cover a Wide Range of Applications – The ATS library covers applications ranging from word processing and page layout to spreadsheets, graphics arts, design, engineering, and Small/Home Office programs.

Optimize Test Page Design – ATSs offer three types of test pages: progressive complexity, real-world and mechanical, to create a complete and diverse testing environment and fully exercise the printable features of each application.

Automate Your Testing - The TestJob Sender automation tool, included with each ATS, manages the flow of test files to your target platform. It automates key tasks, such as performance measurement, cycling the power on hardware, test scheduling, and reporting.

3.3.4. Interop Analyzers

PDF 2.0 and Office Open XML Interop Analyzers validate your device's ability to handle these formats as they are currently used today. We also include files we've developed to use the full capabilities of the latest releases of popular applications.

Interop Analyzers include thousands of test files and a SQL database with the test files' key characteristics so you can search for specific features and attributes. The Interop Analyzer's Query Builder application lets you create custom test suites and add your own files.

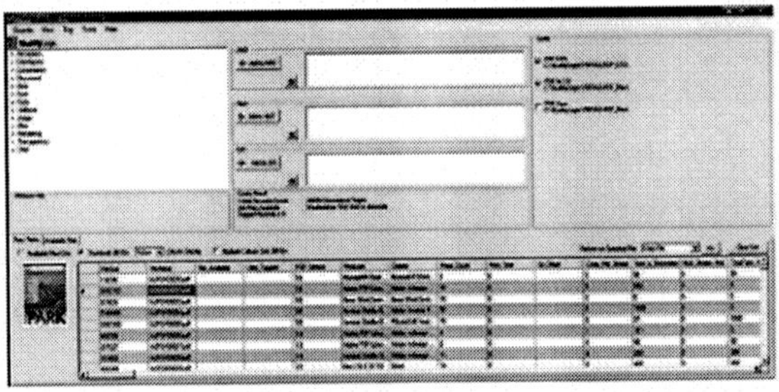

3.3.5. PDL Test Services

Quality Logic can provide full PDL testing services using all of these tools. We work with you as an extension of your engineering or QA group, or we can provide complete QA outsourcing at our facility or yours.

You'll get a full report of where and why your PDL implementation falls short of compliance or fails to work with software applications. We also include our recommendations for fixes.

Choose Quality Logic testing services and you get access to world-class tools and capabilities. Our business is testing, and we bring our leading-edge skills and best practices to any testing problem. We will help you achieve the quality, cost, and schedule goals of your products.

3.4. ADOBE PDF

Adobe Acrobat is a family of application software and Web services developed by Adobe Inc. to view, create, manipulate, print and manage files in Portable Document Format (PDF).

The family comprises Acrobat Reader (formerly Reader), Acrobat (formerly Exchange) and Acrobat.com. The basic Acrobat Reader, available for several desktop and mobile platforms, is freeware; it supports viewing, printing and annotating of PDF files. Additional, "Premium", services are available for reader on paid subscription. The commercial proprietary Acrobat, available for Microsoft Windows and macOS only, can also create, edit, convert, digitally sign, encrypt, export and publish PDF files. Acrobat.com complements the family with a variety of enterprise content management and file hosting services.

3.4.1. Purpose

The main function of Adobe Acrobat is creating, viewing, and editing PDF documents. It can import popular document and image formats and save them as PDF. It is also possible to import a scanner's output, a website, or the contents of the Windows clipboard.

Because of the nature of the PDF, however, once a PDF document is created, its natural organization and flow cannot be meaningfully modified. In other words, Adobe Acrobat is able to modify the contents of paragraphs and images, but doing so does not repaginate the whole document to accommodate for a longer or shorter document. Acrobat can crop PDF pages, change their order, manipulate hyperlinks, digitally sign a PDF file, add comments, redact certain parts of the PDF file, and ensure its adherence to such standards as PDF/A.

Adobe Acrobat came to being in 1993 and had to compete with other products and proprietary formats that aimed to create digital documents:

- Common Ground from No Hands Software Inc.
- Envoy from WordPerfect Corporation
- Folio Views from NextPage
- Replica from Farallon Computing
- WorldView from Interleaf
- DjVu from AT&T Laboratories

Adobe has renamed the Acrobat products several times, in addition to merging, splitting and discontinuing them. Initially, the offered products were called Acrobat Reader,

Acrobat Exchange and Acrobat Distiller. "Acrobat Exchange" soon became "Acrobat". Over time, "Acrobat Reader" became "Reader". Between versions 3 and 5, Acrobat did not have several editions.[clarification needed] In 1999, the Acrobat.com service came to being and introduced several web services whose names started with "Acrobat", but eventually, "Acrobat.com" was downgraded from the name of the family of services, to that of one of those services.

By April 1, 2015, the Acrobat family consisted of:

- Acrobat XI Pro (for Windows and macOS)
- Acrobat XI Standard (for Windows only)
- Reader XI (for Windows, macOS, Android and iOS)
- FormsCentral (web service with desktop client)
- EchoSign (web service)
- Acrobat.com (web service)
- PDF Pack (web service)
- Send (web service)

Unlike most other Adobe products, such as members of Adobe Creative Suite family, the Acrobat products do not have icons that display two letters on a colored rectangle.

Adobe PDF

Adobe Acrobat Reader DC software is the free global standard for reliably viewing, printing, and commenting on PDF documents.

And now, it's connected to the Adobe Document Cloud " making it easier than ever to work across computers and mobile devices.

It's the only PDF viewer that can open and interact with

all types of PDF content, including forms and multimedia.

3.4.2. Adobe Photoshop

Are you not currently a Photoshop user? Adobe offers a Photoshop 30-day trial that you can download right now and it will provide you with plenty of time to learn how it works. If you don't want to eventually purchase Photoshop because it's too expensive, much of what we're going to discuss in these lessons will apply to not just to Photoshop but pretty much most of the standard photo-editing and design tools you'll find (Pixelmator is a great $30 alternative on the Mac, and GIMP is a free, open-source cross-platform option). We've chosen Photoshop because it's the most commonly used, but you're welcome to follow along using other software as well. Today's lesson is pretty Photoshop-specific, but as we move along you should be able to use other software to do most of what we discuss. Ready? Let's get started.

3.4.3. The Toolbar

We're not going to take a look at every single tool but we are going to look at almost every one of them. While this overview will give you an idea of what each tool does, go find yourself a photo and start playing around with them.

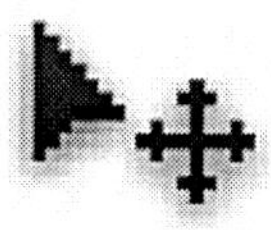

Move Tool (Keyboard: V)

The move tool simply lets you move objects in a given layer around the Photoshop canvas. To use it, click anywhere on the canvas and drag. As you drag, the Photoshop layer will move with your mouse.

Marquee (Keyboard: M)

The marquee lets you select part of the canvas in a specific shape. By default you get a rectangular (or perfect square if you hold down shift while selecting), but you can also select in the shape of an ellipse (or a perfect circle if you hold down shift while selecting).

Lasso (Keyboard: L)

The lasso is a free-form selection tool that lets you drag around the canvas and select anything the lasso'd area covers. Within this tool you also have access to the polygonal lasso, which lets you create a selection by clicking around on the canvas and creating points, and the magnetic lasso, which works the same as the regular lasso but attempts to detect edges for you and automatically snap to them.

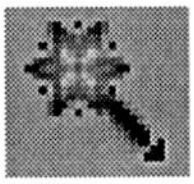

Magic Wand (Keyboard: W)

Clicking an area with the magic wand will tell Photoshop to select the spot you clicked on and anything around it that's similar. This tool can be used as a crude way to remove backgrounds from photos.

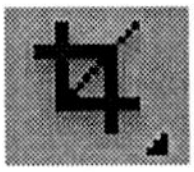

Crop Tool (Keyboard: C)

The crop tool is used to (surprise!) crop your pictures. You can specify the exact size and constrain the crop tool to those proportions, or you can just crop to any size you please.

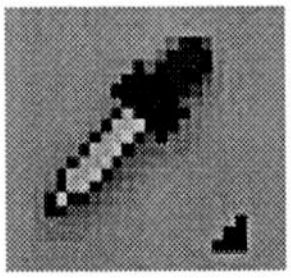

Eyedropper (Keyboard: I)

The eyedropper tool lets you click on any part of the canvas and sample the color at that exact point. The eyedropper will change your foreground color to whatever color it sampled from the canvas.

Healing Brush (Keyboard: J)

The healing brush lets you sample part of the photograph and use it to paint over another part. Once you're finished, Photoshop will examine surrounding areas and try to blend what you painted in with the rest of the picture.

Paintbrush and Pencil (Keyboard: B)

The paintbrush is a tool that emulates a paintbrush and the pencil is a tool that emulates a pencil. The paintbrush, however, can be set to many different kinds of brushes. You can paint with standard paintbrush and airbrush styles, or even paint with leaves and other shapes as well.

Clone Stamp (Keyboard: S)

Like the healing brush, the clone stamp lets you sample part of the photograph and use it to paint over another part. With the clone stamp, however, that's it. Photoshop doesn't do anything beyond painting one area over a new area.

History Brush (Keyboard: Y)

The history brush lets you paint back in time. Photoshop keeps track of all the moves you make (well, 50 by default) and the history brush lets you paint the past back into the current photo. Say you brightened up the entire photo but you wanted to make a certain area look like it did before you brightened it, you can take the history brush and paint that area to bring back the previous darkness.

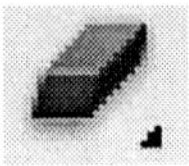

Eraser Tool (Keyboard: E)

The erase tool is almost identical to the paintbrush, except it erases instead of paints.

Paint Can and Gradient Tools (Keyboard: G)

The paint can tool lets you fill in a specific area with the current foreground color. The gradient tool will, by default, create a gradient that blends the foreground and background tool (though you can load and create preset gradients as well, some of which use than two colors).

Blur, Sharpen, and Smudge Tools (Keyboard: None)

All three of these tools act like paintbrushes, but each has a different impact on your picture. The blur tool will blur the area where you paint, the sharpen tool will sharpen it, and the smudge tool will smudge the area all around the canvas. The smudge tool is very useful in drawing for creating nicely blended colors or for creating wisps and smoke that you can add to your photos.

3.4.4. Color Selection Tools (Keyboard: D for defaults, X to switch foreground and background colors)

These tools let you manage the colors you are using. The color on top is the foreground color and the color in back is the background color. The foreground color is what your brushes will use. The background color is what will be used if you delete something from the background or extend it (although now, Photoshop CS$_5$will give you the option for using your foreground color instead in some circumstances). The two smallericons up top are shortcut functions. The left one, showing a black square on a white square, will set yourforeground and background colors to the defaults (Keyboard: D). The double-headed curved arrow willswap your foreground and background color (Keyboard: X). Clicking on either the foreground orbackground color will bring up a color picker so you can set them to precisely the color you want.

Palettes : Palettes are the things that you see sitting over on the right side of your screen. They make it easy for you tonavigate through your document, add adjustments, switch modes, and other things.

Layers : The layers palette lets you see all the layers in your document. As you start getting to know Photoshop, you'll find yourself in this palette more than any other. It'll let you organize and arrange your layers, setblending modes, set visibility and opacity of layers, group and merge layers, and a bunch of other neatthings we'll learn about in future lessons.

Adjustments : Your adjustments panel is where you can easily create and edit adjustment layers. Adjustment layers arenon-destructive image alterations that affect all the layers below them and can easily be turned on and off. Their most common use is for color correction (namely the Levels andCurves adjustments, but there aremany different kinds of adjustments you can perform that can dramatically alter the look of your image.

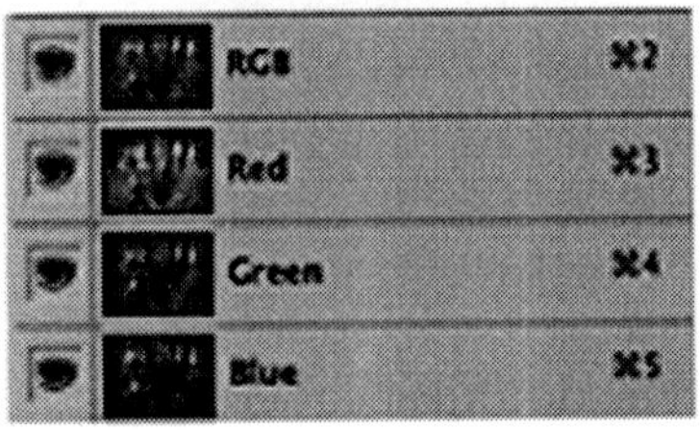

Color Channels : The color channels palette will let you look at the specific colors that make up your picture. If you're inRGB mode you'll get red, green, and blue. These color channels will differ if you're in a different color space(such as CMYK or LAB). When you choose a specific color, you'll notice you'll be shown your image indifferent versions of black and white. This is because each color channel is simply a monochromatic imagesrepresenting the light in each channel (e.g. the red channel is just a look at the red light in your photo). Switching between these different channels is useful for making color channel-specific touch ups, overallcontrast enhancements, and also for converting your photo to black and white in a compelling way. Thiswill be discussed in greater detail in a later lesson about color correction and photo enhancements.

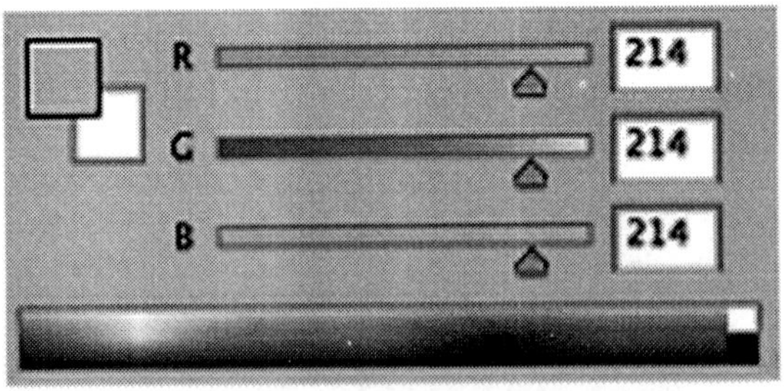

Color Picker : This palette will let you easily alter your foreground and background colors using sliders.

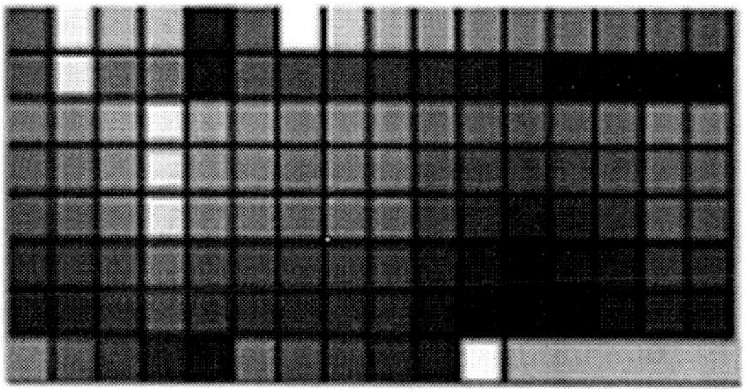

Color Swatches : The color swatches palette is a set of pre-defined colors you can quickly choose from. You can load inseveral other pre-made swatch collections or create your own, too.

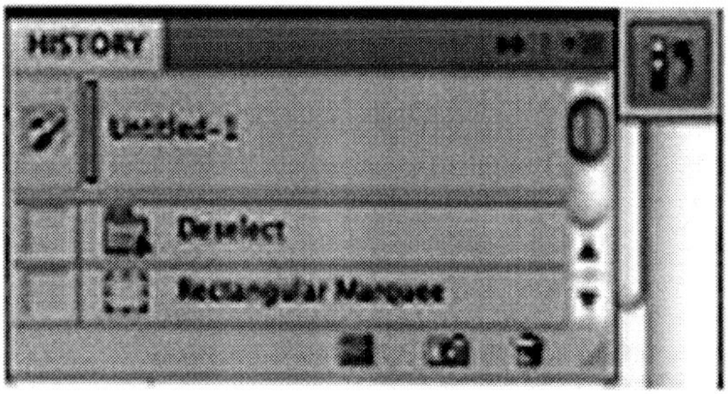

History : The history palette lets you go back in time to undo any previous alterations. The standard undo command(in the edit menu) will simply toggle between undoing and redoing the latest action performed on yourimage. The history panel is where you can go back much further (50 actions by default).

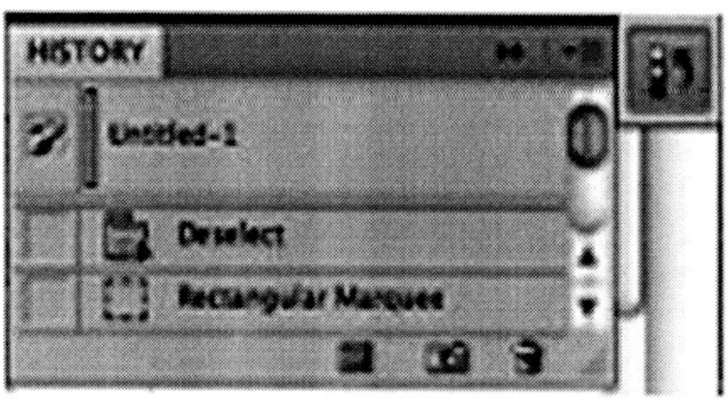

Text : The text palette, and the paragraph palette below it, let you make all sorts of adjustments to any text you create with the type tool. These options are very similar to what you'll find in a word processing, but you can also specify things like character width and spacing which are more useful in design.

Menus : Most of what you'll find in Photoshop's menus can be found using the previously discussed tools. Nonetheless, we're going to take a quick look at some notable items in each of the menus.

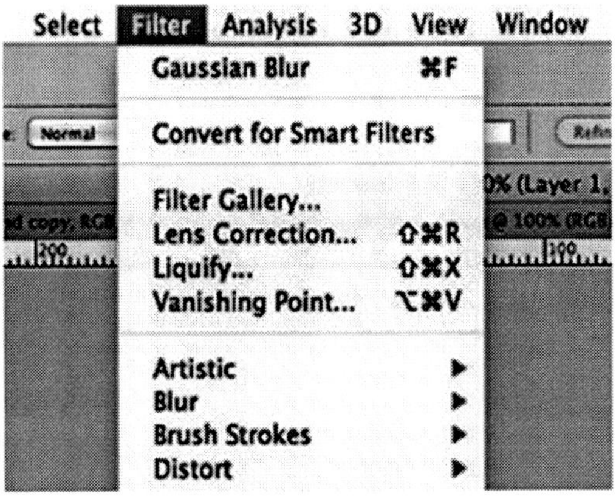

File : File, as usual, handles opening, saving, and closing operations. Towards the end of these lessons we'll be taking a look at your different saving options (namely Save for Web).

Edit : Edit, as usual, brings you copy, cut, and paste. In Photoshop, it's also where you transform layers and setyour color spaces.

Image : Image brings you canvas and image adjustments, including destructive effects that you'll also find in your adjustments palette. Options in this menu are designed to affect the image as a whole, although many adjustments are applied to only a single layer.

Layer : Layer lets you do all of the things you can do in the layer palette with a few more options. This menu alsolets you create adjustment layers and smart objects (a group of layers treated as a single object).

Select : While the marquee and lasso tools will be your main means of selecting things, the select menu can helpyou refine that selection or create entirely new selections based on certain criteria (such as color range andluminosity).

Filter : Filter brings you a wealth of built-in (and, if installed, third-party) Photoshop filters that can blur, sharpen,distort, and alter your image (or layers of the image) in many different and unique ways. The best way toget acquainted with these filters is to try them all. That can take a little time, but it's fun to play aroundwith them and see what they do. We'll be getting into the specifics in subsequent lessons, but only lookingat a few commonly useful filters.

Analysis : Analysis provides you with measurement tools. There will be times when you need them to make accuratealterations to your images. We will not be covering anything in this menu in these basic lessons.

3D : As previously noted, we're not covering 3D. If you decide to learn more about 3D later, you may want toexplore this menu on your own at some point.

View: View provides you with various view options, lets you hide and show line guides you've created, and make Photoshop snap (or not snap) to corners, edges, and to the grid on the canvas. Viewing of this invisible grid can also be turned on and off in the View menu.

Window : Window lets you hide and show certain windows and palettes. You can also arrange your Photoshop windows and palettes however you want and save them as a window preset.

Legacy Document : Legacy documents include all of the important records that every business must retain – records like incorporation papers, tax returns, partnership agreements, contracts, and other legal documents that need to be preserved and maintained for business continuity and corporate history. Many of these documents are maintained as paper files, taking up space, risking deterioration, and sometimes proving to be difficult to find in old filing systems.

While there are paper storage companies that are dedicated to the premise that paper storage can be safe, secure and permanent, the truth is that paper is paper and it does deteriorate. Not only that, but paper document storage takes up huge amounts of space, and the physical real estate needed to store paper can be costly.

3.5. ANALOG TO DIGITAL

Analog-to-Digital Converters, (ADCs) allow micro-processor controlled circuits, Arduinos, Raspberry Pi, and other such digital logic circuits to communicate with the real world. In the real world, analogue signals have continuously changing values which come from various sources and sensors which can measure sound, light, temperature or movement, and many digital systems interact with their environment by measuring the analogue signals from such transducers.

While analogue signals can be continuous and provide an infinite number different voltage values, digital circuits on the other hand work with binary signal which have only two discrete states, a logic "1" (HIGH) or a logic "0" (LOW). So it is necessary to have an electronic circuit which can convert between the two different domains of continuously changing analogue signals and discrete digital signals, and this is where Analogue-to-Digital Converters (A/D) come in.

Basically an analogue to digital converter takes a snapshot of an analogue voltage at one instant in time and produces a digital output code which represents this analogue voltage. The number of binary digits, or bits used to represent this analogue voltage value depends on the resolution of an A/D converter.

For example a 4-bit ADC will have a resolution of one part in 15, (24 – 1) whereas an 8-bit ADC will have a resolution of one part in 255, (28 – 1). Thus an analogue to digital converter takes an unknown continuous analogue signal and converts it into an "n" - bit binary number of 2n bits.

But first let us remind ourselves of the differences between an analogue (or analog) signal and a digital signal as shown:

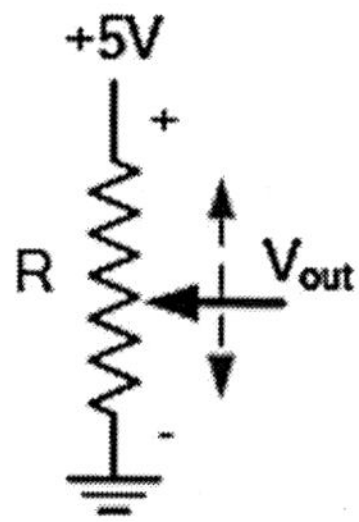

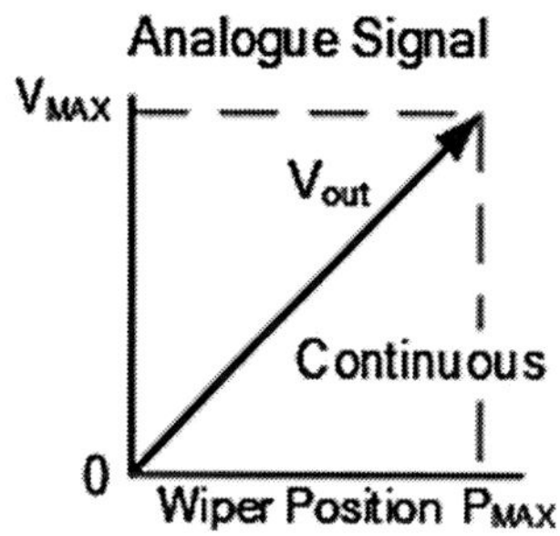

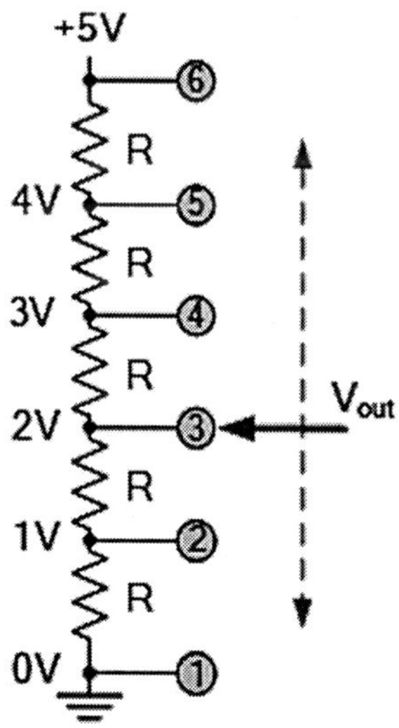

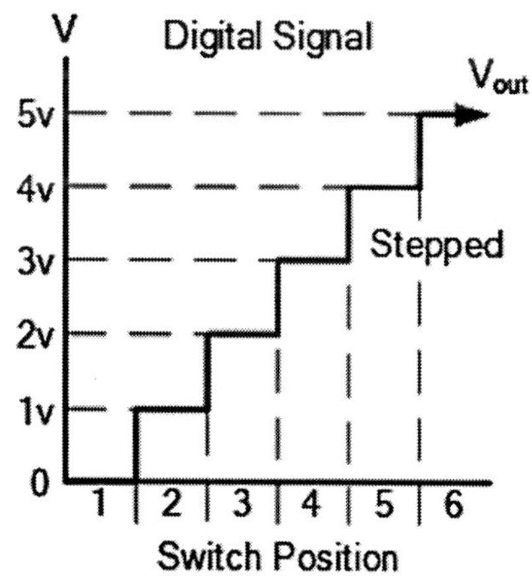

Here we can see that as the wiper terminal of the potentiometer is rotated between between 0 volts and VMAX, it produces a continuous output signal (or voltage) which has an infinite number of output values relative to the wiper position. As the potentiometers wiper is adjusted from one position to the next, there is no sudden or step change between the two voltage levels thereby producing a continuously variable output voltage. Examples of analogue signals include temperature, pressure, liquid levels and light intensity.

For a digital circuit the potentiometer wiper has been replaced by a single rotary switch which is connected in turn to each junction of the series resistor chain, forming a basic potential divider network. As the switch is rotated from one position (or node) to the next the output voltage, VOUT changes quickly in discrete and distinctive voltage steps representing multiples of 1.0 volts on each switching action or step as shown.

So for example, the output voltage will be 2 volts, 3 volts, 5 volts, etc. but NOT 2.5V, 3.1V or 4.6V. Finer output voltage levels could easily be produced by using a multi-positional switch and increasing the number of resistive elements within the potential divider network, therefore increasing the number of discrete switching steps.

Then we can see that the major differences between an analogue signal and a digital signal is that an "Analogue" quantity is continuously changing over time while a "Digital" quantity has discrete (step by step) values. "LOW" to "HIGH" or "HIGH" to "LOW". So how can we convert a continously changing signal with an infinite number of values to one which has distinct values or steps for use by a digital circuit.

Analog-to-Digital Converter

The process of taking an analogue voltage signal and converting it into an equivalent digital signal can be done in many different ways, and while there are many analogue-to-digital converter chips such as the ADC08xx series available from various manufacturers, it is possible to build a simple ADC using discrete components. One simple and easy way is by using parallel encoding, also known as flash, simultaneous, or multiple comparator converters in which comparators are used to detect different voltage levels and output their switching state to an encoder.

Parallel of "Flash" A/D converters use a series of interconnected but equally spaced comparators and voltage references generated by a series network of precision resistors for generating an equivalent output code for a particular n-bit resolution. The advantage of parallel or flash converters is that they are simple to construct and do not require any timing clocks as the instant an analogue voltage is applied to the comparator inputs, it is compared against a reference voltage.

3.5.1. Conversion from Analog to Digital

Analog-to-Digital converters (ADC) translate analog signals, real world signals like temperature, pressure, voltage, current, distance, or light intensity, into a digital representation of that signal. This digital representation can then be processed, manipulated, computed, transmitted or stored.

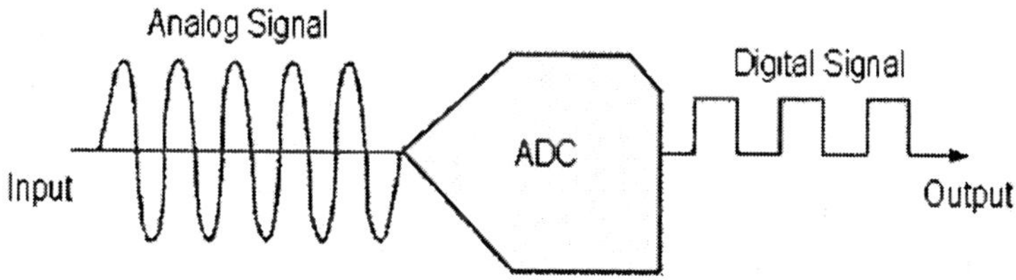

Analog to Digital Conversion

In many cases, the analog to digital conversion process is just one step within a larger measurement and control loop where digitized data is processed and then reconverted back to analog signals to drive external transducers. These transducers can include things like motors, heaters and acoustic divers like loudspeakers. The performance required of the ADC will reflect the performance goals of the measurement and control loop. ADC performance needs will also reflect the capabilities and requirements of the other signal processing elements in the loop.

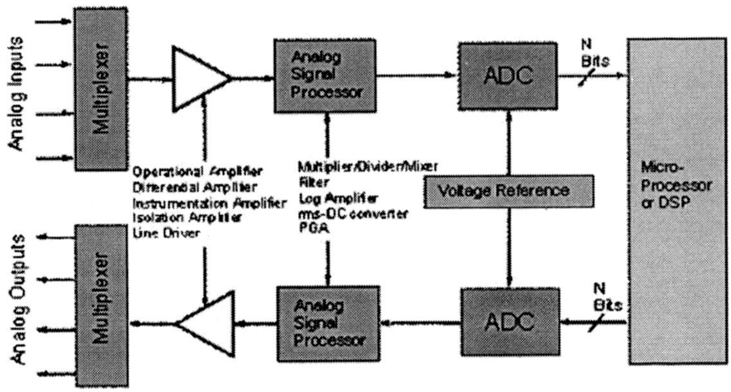

Measurement and Control Loop

3.5.2. Basic Operation

An ADC samples an analog waveform at uniform time intervals and assigns a digital value to each sample. The digital value appears on the converter's output in a binary coded format. The value is obtained by dividing the sampled analog input voltage by the reference voltage and them multiplying by the number of digital codes. The resolution of converter is set by the number of binary bits in the output code.

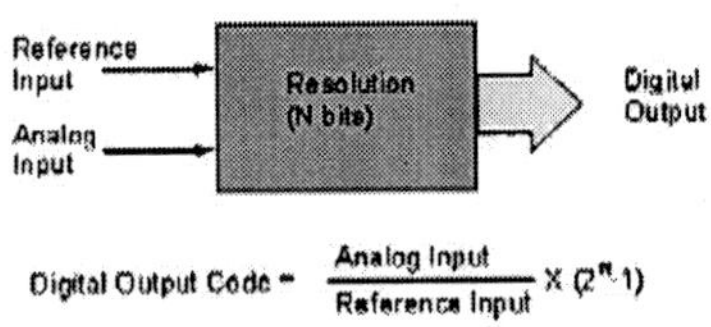

Digital output code

An ADC carries out two processes, sampling and quantization. The ADC represents an analog signal, which has infinite resolution, as a digital code that has finite resolution. The ADC produces 2N digital values where N represents the number of binary output bits. The analog input signal will fall between the quantization levels because the converter has finite resolution resulting in an inherent uncertainty or quantization error. That error determines the maximum dynamic range of the converter.

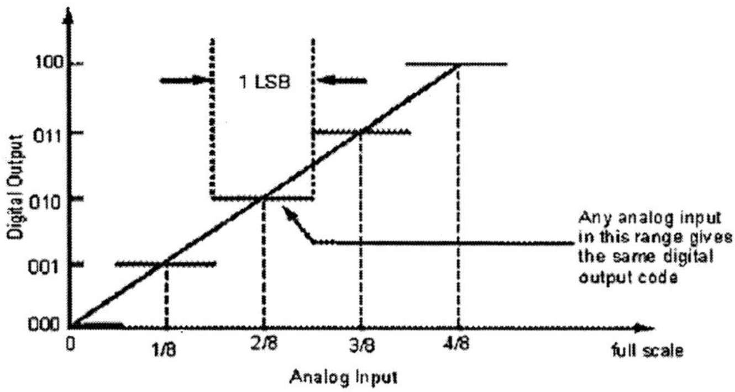

Quantization Process

The sampling process represents a continuous time domain signal with values measured at discrete and uniform time intervals. This process determines the maximum bandwidth of the sampled signal in accordance with the NY Quist Theory. This theory states that the signal frequency must be less than or equal to one half the sampling frequency to prevent aliasing. Aliasing is a condition in which frequency signals outside the desired signal band will, through the sampling process, appear within the bandwidth of interest. However, this aliasing process can be exploited in communications systems design to down-convert a high frequency signal to a lower frequency. This technique is known as under-sampling. A criterion for under-sampling is that the ADC has sufficient input bandwidth and dynamic range to acquire the highest frequency signal of interest.

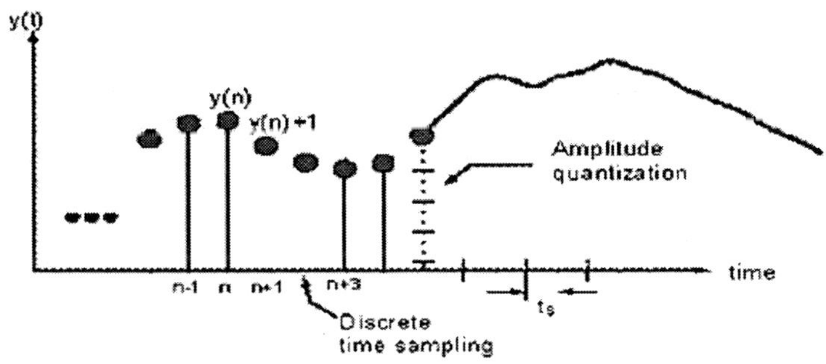

Sampling Process

Sampling and quantization are important concepts because they establish the performance limits of an ideal ADC. In an ideal ADC, the code transitions are exactly 1 least significant bit (LSB) apart. So, for an N-bit ADC, there are 2N codes and 1 LSB = FS/2N, where FS is the full-scale analog input voltage. However, ADC operation in the real world is also affected by non-ideal effects, which produce errors beyond those dictated by converter resolution and sample rate. These errors are reflected in a number of AC and DC performance specifications associated with ADCs.

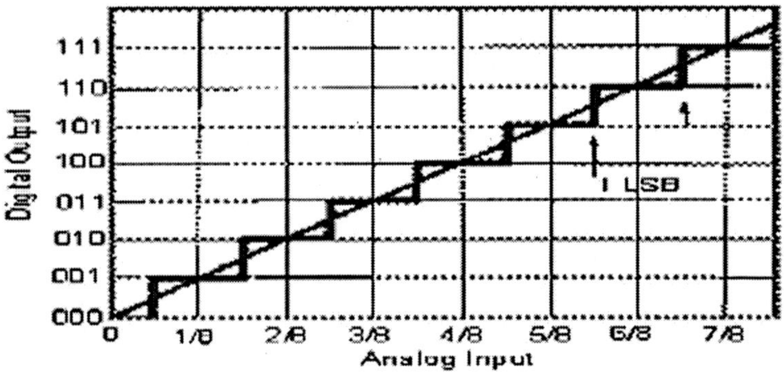

Transfer Function for an Ideal ADC

Any analog input in this range gives the same digital output code.

Adobe Acrobat Export PDF supports optical character recognition, or OCR, when you convert a PDF file to Word (.doc and .docx), Excel (.xlsx), or RTF (rich text format). OCR is the conversion of images of text (scanned text) into editable characters, so that you can search, correct, and copy the text.

When OCR is enabled, Adobe Acrobat Export PDF performs OCR on PDF files that contain images, vector art, hidden text, or a combination of these elements. (For example, Adobe Acrobat Export PDF performs OCR on PDF files created from scanned documents.) Adobe Acrobat Export PDF also performs OCR on text that it can't interpret because the text was encoded incorrectly in the source application.

3.5.3. Supported languages

Adobe Acrobat Export PDF supports the following languages for OCR:

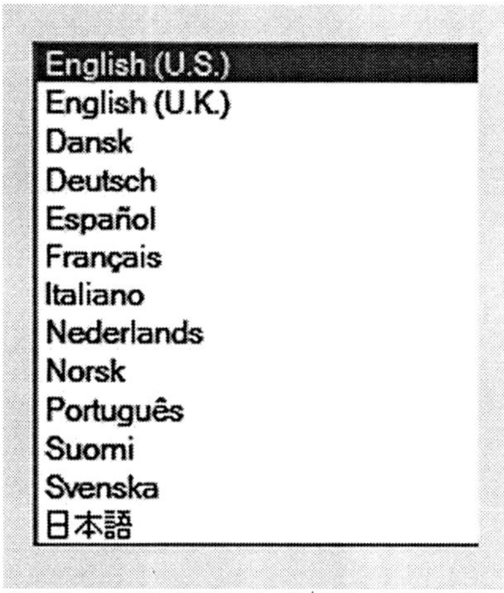

By default, OCR uses the language selected in the My Information dialog box. The OCR engine uses the selected language to interpret the scanned text. Selecting the correct language improves the accuracy of the conversion, as the OCR engine uses language-specific dictionaries for conversion. For non-Latin languages like Japanese, the OCR engine cannot interpret and convert the text unless you've selected the appropriate language.

Using Acrobat Export PDF web interface

To perform OCR when you convert a PDF file in Adobe Acrobat Export PDF, do the following:

1. Log in to Adobe Acrobat Export PDF, and click Select PDF files to Export.
2. Click Choose Files from My Computer and browse to your PDF. Also, you can drag a file on the pane. For selecting a file from Document Cloud, click Document Cloud in the left pane and then select your file.

   NOTE: You can select multiple files for export.

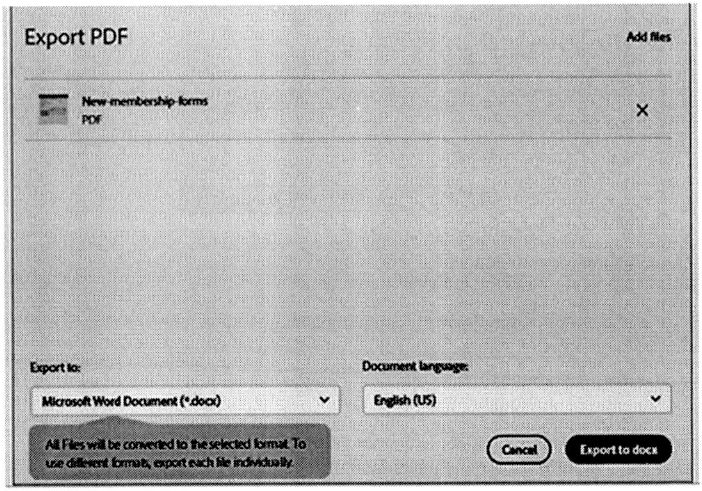

3. In the **Export To** drop-down list, select the format to which you want to export the PDF.
4. In the **Document Language** drop-down list, select an appropriate document language for text recognition.
5. Click the **Export to <format>** button for exporting the content.
6. The selected PDF file is uploaded to the server and the content is exported to the desired format. Click the **Download** icon to save the file on your computer or device.

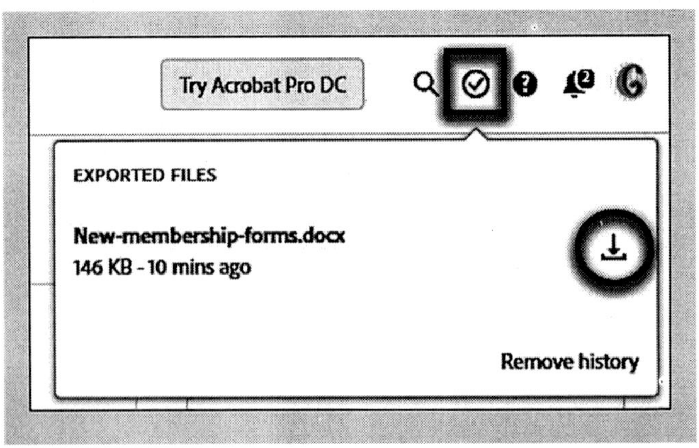

The free Adobe Scan app turns your device into a powerful portable scanner that recognizes text automatically (OCR). Capture new images with your camera or grab any image from your device. The app converts images to PDF and saves them to Adobe Document Cloud. By default, the app automatically converts image text to real text via optical character recognition (OCR).

Scan features include:

Scanning: Quick steps

Device settings

Scanning from the capture window

- Optional steps
- Document types

Importing from your gallery

Edit your scan

Add photos to existing scans

Reorder pages

Crop pages

Rotate pages

Adjust the color

Cleanup the image

Delete pages

Canceling a scan or edit

Save as PDF

Live edge boundary detection

Quick actions

3.6. SUMMARY

We have seen how Photoshop can be used to create simple animated images. Now it is up to you to explore the possibilities further. Animations should be used on a web page to create interest or convey a message. The animation should not be used as an end uto itself – to draw attention to it so the viewer thinks "Oh what a clever animated image. I wonder why it is there?" Animations should be used sparingly or they will defeat their purpose.

Different type of ADCs architectures are studied and analyzed various designing constraints speed, conversion time, sampling Rate, Resolution Power dissipation and Area Occupied. The objective is to design ADCs by using specific technology by which there ADCs are implemented in various applications with low power dissipation and less area occupation.

3.7. REVIEW QUESTION

1. Describe the Conversion from Analog to Digital?
2. Define Photoshop ?
3. Define OCR software?

Unit 4

OBJECTIVES

- To learn about Electronic Publishing
- To provide access to information to E-journals and e-books
- To implement new IT processes to provide high quality information.

4.1. INTRODUCTION

Information is an intellectual resource that has the capacity to change the image of society. Consequently, large investments are being made by the government all over the world on the information technology industry for generating, processing and disseminating the information. Most of the scientific research literature today is coming on an array of information resources, such as floppies, magnetic tapes, internet, websites, CD ROMs, the outgrowth of advances in computer and communication technology. They are becoming more popular for accessing, retrieval and offering services electronically, replacing gradually their print counterparts. During the last three decades, the information formats and delivery systems have changed considerably. Internet is emerging as a very powerful tool to make information quickly available on the network to all potential users located anywhere. Internet documents have the quality of all time accessibility. Timely delivery of extremely current information has always been a crucial factor in special libraries. Moreover, such libraries have always dealt with a diverse range of non-book information and material, most of which are inherently suited to electronic format.

Electronic publishing is the dissemination of information in electronic formats and its distribution to potential users either on electronic networks such as the Internet and intranet or in stand-alone formats such as CD ROMs and diskette.

E-publishing has been defining as any non-print media material that is published in digitized form to an identifiable public. The media in electronic publishing can be text, numeric, graphic, still or motion pictures, video, sound or as infrequently the case a combination of any or all of these.

E-publishing can be represented as [highlight] Electronic publishing = Electronic technology + computer technology + communication technology + publishing. [/ highlight]

Electronic publishing (e-publishing) deals with the collection, modification, and distribution of information, art, and software in any form, such as on physical media or via computer networks. E-publishing may be broadly divided into two categories: online and offline publishing. Online publishing uses computer and communication networks including the Internet, intranet, and extranet for delivery of the content. Offline publishing uses storage media such as CD ROM, CD-I, DVD, memory card and diskette for distributing the content. By definition, an electronic publication (e-publication) is the publication of any form of electronic media.

4.2. DEFINITIONS OF ELECTRONIC PUBLISHING

According to F.W. Lancaster, "Electronic publishing is a publication process where the manuscripts are submitted in electronic format, edited, printed, and even distributed to readers (users) in electronic form by employing computer and telecommunication technology."

"The production of the document in computer-readable form for distribution over a computer network or in other formats such as CD ROMS." "Electronic publishing is electronic commerce in digital goods and services that are intended for consumption by human sense"

4.3. NEED OF THE ELECTRONIC PUBLISHING

The exponential growth in publishing has resulted in greater difficulty in retrieving information from libraries and other sources due to the existing literature being widely scattered. The need to reduce the time required in conventional publishing and the realization of the potential and unique feature of electronic media are some of the reason which has resulted in the shift of emphasis from conventional publishing to electronic publishing. There are four main reasons for the development of e-publishing,

- Rapid development and wide use of computer technology.
- The tremendous growth of computer networks.
- Merging of computer and telecommunication technology.
- Development of information industry.

The process of c publishing is done through electro copying. Electro copying is a process of converting printed material into an electronic form, this is achieved by scanning the printed material into an electronic database in which the text is stored in either image or character encoded form by means of a scanning technique.

4.4. EVALUATION OF ELECTRONIC PUBLISHING

In the year 1455, Johannes Gutenberg invented his famous printing press with movable type. And the first book "Gutenberg 42-line Bible" was produced by Gutenberg's printing press. The technology was enabled the manufacture of high quality printed documents at a fraction of the cost of hand-copying. This invention had changed the printing scenario and is considered as a landmark. After a few decades, in 1490, Aldus Manutius founded the Aldine Press in Venice. There were many changes and many printing presses came into existence to start printing documents. Out of them remarkably, Abraham Ortelius produced the first modern atlas - Theatrum Orbis Terrarum in 1570 and slowly such productions could get the commercial advantages, contributors and associates started to earn. It is found that Alexander Pope, translator of the Iliad became the overpaid author in 1720.

The second landmark in this area as found in the production of Wood pulp paper commercially for the first time in 1840. During this period, typesetting was done manually by hand at a rate of about 2000 letters per hour. In 1883, Tolbert Langston invented the first mechanical typesetting machine, called monotype. With monotype, letters were set at 6000 per hour.

In the last century, as it is found, the work of H G Wells had got importance. He wrote the 'World Brain' in 1938. The World Brain is Wells' vision of a vast print encyclopedia of all human knowledge whose production company would become a new institution for knowledge and education. In 1945, Vannevar Bush wrote an essay to describe a device called the `memex'. The `memex' was the size of a desk to store books and other materials on microfilm and had the ability to link and connect passages among documents. Another important invention in the twentieth century probably as Hypertext.

The term 'Hypertext' was coined by Ted Nelson in 1965. Ted Nelson wrote also about his utopian project Xanadu in which all the works of the world are permanently stored in a universally accessible repository. In the same year (1965 AD) Marshall McLuhan, media prophet, predicted the coming impact and potential profit of the merging of electronic technology and books, as by that time the digital computer came into existence already, and the emergence of computer technology with the printing was started in the form of word processing. In 1968, Alan Kay created a cardboard model of the Dynabook – a computer with a million-pixel screen. This was basically a visionary device, which Kay claimed as something more like super-paper. In 1971, the project `Gutenberg' started to create a free Computer classics Library at the University of Illinois with the leadership of Michael Hart after he wrote the 'Declaration of Independence'. At the end of 2001, the Gutenberg collection has crossed the 10000 titles. In 1979, Doug Adams released the popular science fiction novel, `The Hitchhiker's Guide to the Galaxy', in which protagonist Ford Perfect researches the galaxy for a vast electronic book called The Hitchhiker's Guide. The Random House Electronic Thesaurus is arguably the world's first commercially available 'Electronic Book' (e-Book), which is published in 1981. This is another landmark for today's e-publishing. In 1986, Franklin Electronic Publishers embedded an electronic dictionary in a handheld device, producing the first portable e-Book. Barnes & Noble opened its first superstore in 1990. Sony's Data Disernan was designed to display CD-ROM books on a 3.5-inch screen in 1991. With the blessings of the Internet, e-publishing has got a new dimension. In 1995, Amazon.com began selling print books on the web. In 2000, the availability of Microsoft Reader with a clear type launched a new era of reading on screen. Recently, the map-book becomes an e-Book when the Library of Congress American Memory Project digitized the seventy maps and presented them on the web!

4.4.1. Categories of E-Publishing

Electronic publishing can be categorized into two ways.

1. Offline
2. On- line

In off-line publishing information is entirely passes into the possession of the purchaser or user, who can access it an unlimited number of times without any further change. For example computer software or reference material on compact disc in a physically tangible and transportable form. In can be accessed repeatedly using an electronic reader like a personal computer or compact disc player.

In online publishing, the information remains in a publisher controlled computer, usually accessible only on payment of a fee for each use. Unlike off-line publishing on-line publishing can be continuously updated, managed and refined. In off-line publishing, the publisher has no way to quickly update the database. So new editions or supplements must be periodically distributed to each user.

4.4.2. Types of E-Publishing

1. E-Journal.
2. E-Book.

3. E-Database.
4. E-Thesis and dissertation.
5. E-Archive and back file.
6. Bulletin boards.
7. Multimedia resources etc.

4.4.3. Advantages of E-Publishing

Following are the main of e-publishing:

1. Maintenance of updated information : Data can maintain aptitude so that the buyer will be able to purchase the latest version of publication.

2. On-demand publishing: The individual subscribers can be provided with only those documents, which match their profile, and can be charged accordingly. 'On-demand publishing' also allows retrospective searching and SDI.

3. Information retrieval Just in time : Library and Information Centers do not 'buy publication' to access the information in it, they can have online access to the E-Journals and download or print the required material. EP provides aids for connectivity, audio visualization customizability, creation and revision of documents, interactivity and rapid information retrieval.

4. Speed : Publication of E-Journals saves the turn-around time, i.e., the time lag in submission, referring, vision, editing, composing, printing, binding, and forwarding, which is eliminated by using computer and communication networks. This enhances timely publication and is suitable to the letters-type journals where rapid communication is of utmost importance. This leads to further reducing the gap between the author and the end-user.

5. Distribution: The major advantages of e-journals are their global distribution, their hyperlinks, and the ability to access different sites and the ability to search.

6. Retrieval : There are a good number of search engines available to access and retrieve the appropriate articles. Most of the publishers of E-journals are providing keywords, author searches, terms reducing the role of additional indexing and abstracting.

7. Multiple Accesses : Most of the publishers of E-journals are coming up with site license policy providing multiple accesses and access through the campus LAN.

8. Manageability : Electronic information can easily be managed to be managed by adding bookmarks and personal notes to the sites or by downloading it of private files or databases for copying and editing.

4.4.4. Disadvantages of Electronic Publishing

Some of the disadvantages of e-publishing are as follows:

1. High initial cost : E-Publishing includes high initial costs to the publishers, as well as L & Information Centers, have to invest before benefits are expected.

2. Incompatible Hardware and Software : The non-compatibility of hardware due to the absence of common standards, and the usage of different retrieval software by different publishers. The acceptance of E-journals depends upon the user-friendly retrieval software.

3. Weak Infrastructure of Computer and Communication Network : As a prerequisite, E-Publishing products necessitate the proper availability of a computer and communication network to the subscriber.

4. The gap between Developed and Developing Countries : the gaps between developed and developing countries make the E-publishing an elitist technology.

5. In readability : E-Journal may take some time to percolate down to the reader label mainly due to the problem of displaying page images conveniently on computer screen.

For the entire page to be accommodated the size of the image has to be reduced and the low resolution makes it difficult to read.

6. Inconvenient to use : Ease of use i.e., reading at a convenient time and place, is not possible with EPs.

7. Delay in the release : In many instances, when the publication is issued in both printed and electronic form, the electronic version is released after a gap of three to four weeks.

8. User training : In many instances, when the publication is issued in both printed and electronic form for using the electronic version user training is considered to be very essential as all the users are not well familiar with an electronic form of it.

4.5. ELECTRONIC PUBLISHING AND ITS ROLE IN LIBRARIES

The definition of a library is an *institution* that selects, acquires, organizes, and provides access to record knowledge. This is obviously a very broad definition, but both the collecting ad organizing aspect of librarianship is threatened by electronic publishing.

When it becomes cheaper to offer patrons access to material that is stored *electronically* than on paper, then electronic access will rapidly become accepted, in spite of many limitations it has. One of the primary characteristics of scholarly publishing is that the use of any particular article is fairly low, low enough that it will be probably cheaper to store the material at central sites rather than at each library. In spite of being in electronic form, the amount of material that a typical library acquires in paper form is still a substantial burden. This will push libraries into using central repositories to handle electronic publications is so easy and fast, that the lack of local storage should not be a problem to the users, hardly noticeable, in fact, if the system is properly constructed.

4.6. THE FUTURE FOR ELECTRONIC PUBLISHING IN LIBRARY AND INFORMATION SCIENCE

The foregoing analyses of industry and market trends apply generally to the electronic information industry, of which, as we have seen, library and information science is one part. The data on the number and usage of databases in the field suggest that it is only a small part of the whole, and one which is accorded far less priority from its primary audience-librarians and other information professionals-than are databases serving their clients' needs. There is no significant indication that a shift in priorities on the part of information professionals is forthcoming despite the fact that the professional literature is a primary resource for any field that seeks to respond to both a dynamic external environment and internal pressures to adapt to increasingly complex issues and practices. Thus electronic publishing in library and information science seems destined to play a continual game of catch-up, with information providers in the field applying new techniques and technologies to the professional literature well after they have been applied to the information resources of other fields. The extent to which professionally oriented information products and services succeed in the library and information services marketplace will be one measure of the importance information professionals give themselves at a time of significant technological, environmental, and professional change.

4.7. ELECTRONIC PUBLISHING TECHNOLOGY

The E-Publishing use some of the methods are followed:

Commissioning : The Publishers have long been responsible for commissioning work that they believe to be of publishable quality and that they predict will meet consumer expectations. In most cases the reader can rely on the publisher to provide books that are (for the most part) well written and have some merit. The Internet has, however, provided authors with a place in which to cheaply publish their work, allowing many authors that would ordinarily not have been offered a publishing contract to self-publish their work. It may be argued that this opens the realm of literature to greater freedom of expression and undermines the power of an ultimately profit-driven publishing industry; however it is frequently noted that, 'the Internet is littered with "rubbish"... there is at present a great deal of shallow, inaccurate, poor-quality writing on the Internet' (Roberts 1999)

Peer Review : Authority, validity and quality of writing are also key concerns in the field of scholarly e-publishing, particularly in areas such as medical publishing where incorrect data may lead to potentially dangerous misinformation. Peer review has traditionally helped academic publishers filter out work containing poor-quality and inaccurate data.

Editing and Proofreading : The author–editor relationship, email now allows swift, direct communication and exchange of digital, print-ready files, regardless of authors' geographical location mentioned the details. This drastically reduces the amount of time that books and journals spend in production, and means that publishers can more easily publish the work of authors that are based in remote locations.

Design and Typesetting : Another type of the Desktop publishing has also revolutionaries the role of the designer and typesetter of the electronic publishing.

Printing : E-publishing is the removal of printing from the publishing process in the proof and finally printing the materials.

Sales and Marketing : In the recent years of the world has been direct online book sales allow publishers to sell books directly to the customer and bypass the bookstore, and to this end books are rarely published today without a URL on the cover, directing the reader to the publisher's website.

Format : The some formats, such as the proposed Open eBook standard (OEB) Rocket e-book, and AportisDoc, allow this, while other formats based on Adobe portable document format (pdf) only allow scaling of the page used.

Electronic Books : E – Books are electronic versions of books, which are delivered to consumers in digital formats. There are a large number of devices being developed to make reading e-books easier for consumers. Special software, which makes documents or pages of a book easier to read on a screen, is also being developed by software companies. A standard for E-book software, known as the open-e-book standard, or OEB, has been developed as a standard format for e-books, but competing standards such as Adobe's PDF exist. The potential market for electronic books (and shorter length content) is extremely large. Although presently there is some sales resistance to the idea of abandoning paper books for a handheld electronic reader, certain sectors of the public are already recognizing the benefits of e-books over paper books. Students who are tired of lugging around forty pounds of textbooks (which become obsolete quickly) and consumers or business people who travel a great deal are two groups who seem thrilled with the idea of downloading 10 or more books into a small, portable reader. E-books are already starting to be trendy.

The E-books followed by the technology are listed below:

Print-on-demand (POD) is become comfortable with electronic reading software and e-book reading devices.

Digital content used for delivering digital content includes Adobe PDF, XML, HTML, WAP (Wireless Application Protocol) and other technologies.

Electronic Ink is a developing technology that could have a huge impact on the media and publishing industries in the recent years.

E-Mail Publishing used the ease of delivery and

production of email newsletters has led to the development of a massive number of available email newsletters, mailing lists and discussion lists on a large variety of topics.

Web Publishing used web based content like web programming language, HTML is still the most widely used, but XML is also making headway.

Electronic publishing is electronic journal, which is a full text journal published electronically, and can be accessed on the web. Either an electronic journal can be free or subscription based. Advantages of electronic journal are its ease of access and regular updating, ease of downloading articles, etc. Many publishers now offer electronic journals along with print version with sometimes free access to the electronic journal on subscribing to the print version. An increasing number of journals are now available only electronically whereas online databases are large amounts of information stored in a search tool's website. It refers to information transferred to hard disks, magnetic tape, etc., which are accessed through communication network. Libraries subscribe various types of online database depending on the subject requirements of the academic community. Most of the online databases have a user-friendly search interface to search the database and save the required results for future use.

The following lists of Publishing Software are available and listed to below:

- Adobe In Design
- Adobe PageMaker, was Aldus PageMaker; supplanted by In Design
- QuarkXPress
- Frame Maker, now owned by Adobe
- Green street Publisher Home and Publisher Business
- In Page - DTP which works with English + Urdu, Arabic, Persian, Pashto etc.

- Interleaf/Quicksilver
- iStudio Publisher - Desktop publishing and design software for Mac OS X
- Microsoft Publisher
- Microsoft Word 2008 - This Word release contains a DTP mode
- Pages, by Apple, Inc.
- Page Stream, formerly known as Publishing Partner
- Prefis Book Machine - Early 80s Publishing software that ran on the Apricot
- PC/Xi - output in CORA to Linotron 202.
- Prince XML, by Yes Logic
- Print Shop, originally produced by Broderbund
- RagTime
- Serif PagePlus
- SVG Kit for Adobe Creative Suite is a plug-in, which adds support of SVG files to Adobe In Design
- Ventura Publisher, now owned by Corel and originally developed by Ventura Software
- UltraXML, XML Dynamic Publishing Solution
- Print MIS, Solution provider for the printing industry

4.7.1. Impacts of E-Publishing

Impacts on stakeholders' interrelationships : New entrants in the supply side of the scholarly communication system were enabled by the OA, strongly challenging the relationships among publishers, libraries and authors. Competitiveness has been gradually injected to the market, since the new entrants are now performing some of the scientific publishing functions, such as registering, archiving and dissemination11. The online resources promote a way for authors to increase their work dissemination and its consequent usage and impact. Additionally, the academic actors have been realising that they can assume the performance of some processes in the scholarly communication system, for which they have been actually responsible for years .

Impacts on the publishers-researchers (as authors) interrelationships : The major e-publishing impacts on the publisher-researcher interrelationship have been observed on the controversial issues about copyright ownership and on the inclusion of researchers as the disseminators of their own work in any stage of its development.

In an OA model, the copyright ownership is required to remain with authors or with the institution, which license specific rights to publishers. According to Crow (2002, pp. 21-22) the authors' retention of the copyright and the retention of the right to publish copies of their articles in OA journals or in institutional repositories (IRs) are essential elements of the changes which have being occurring in the scholarly publishing system.

Currently, authors are still dependent on publishers for reusing their own material and for publishing it on the open access models. The authors' recovering of their copyright ownership affects this current relationship of dependence, because instead of assigning total copyright to publishers, authors can assign only specific rights to publishers, using licenses like the Creative Commons. Actually, publishers do not need copyright transfer agreements either to publish or to exploit the article commercially .Therefore, the returning of the copyright ownership to authors' reduces their dependence on publishers freeing them to the dissemination or exploitation of their own research work for educational and commercial purposes.

In addition, the OA strategies have enabled researchers and institutions to become disseminators of their own intellectual production and to breach the distribution channel exclusivity owned by publishers. The dissemination of their own intellectual production can be made in any stage of its development as pre-refereed (pre-print) and refereed published articles (post-print). This has promoted the exchanging of ideas and comments about a work, its informal quality certification, and mainly its wider and free of charge dissemination. These new practices affect the relationship publishers-researchers, since researchers as authors start demanding the possibility to self-archive pre-prints of their work without affecting the possibility having it published further. Additionally, the use of OA journals as a complement to traditional publishers' work can be identified by the growing participation of authors in OA journals, rising from 11% (in January 2004) to 29% (in July 2005).

Within this scenario, the growing of free online scientific content which is resulted from authors' dissemination can pressure traditional publishers to refocus their offerings and to offer more valued services beyond the single content delivery.

Impacts on the publishers-libraries inter-relationships : The publisher-library interrelationship has been affected because with the IRs, libraries are becoming actively involved and heavily responsible for the dissemination and archiving of the research outputs of their institution. All these changes have increased librarians' visibility and promoted a more strategic importance for them inside the institution.

With the growth in adoption and use of IRs libraries have a leading role in the management of IRs since they are responsible for organising, archiving and disseminating the intellectual creation of the institution. It should be remembered that peer-reviewed archives with an efficient search engine perform the functions of journals (Wellcome Trust, 2004, p.24). Consequently, the new position of libraries threats publishers, since they can publish their own scientific work and intermediate the work from other universities.

Within this new context, librarians acquire new roles such as facilitators of some of the attitudinal changes required to support the IR results, and as pointed out by Johnson (2004) and Bosc & Harnad (2005, p.99), librarians acquire the role of promoters of OA journals and self-archiving, including OA resources and services in the library gateways. Additionally, libraries will have more knowledge in relation to the users than publishers will do, because they will continue to be the main gateway for the whole distributed scientific content access.

The publishers-libraries interrelationship has also been affected by users' article-based consumption behaviour. Waltham (2003, p. 10) has pointed out that "readers are interested in smaller units, individual articles" and that they purchase information in smaller units than those in print-based market. This change demands that the negotiation between libraries and publishers be based on articles, rather than on larger packages of information, making libraries budget more flexibly managed. Thus, the publishers-libraries interrelationship should become more flexible and be governed by lower and more manageable costs, because the exchange unit will be based on articles and on the effective combination of articles that can match users' needs and libraries budgets. The article-based consumption will also demand new services (e.g. search tools, citation linking, single interface) from publishers and libraries, influencing on the practice of a more cooperative interrelationship between both.

Impacts on the publishers-users interrelationships : The publisher-user interrelationship has been affected by the increased usage of digital scientific information and user's article-based consumption behaviour. Consequently, users demand convenient access to qualified scientific information and increasingly sophisticated digital services to navigate through and use this information. Moreover, users want "to select and access distilled and well-written arguments" using a common interface without having to access different interfaces from different systems and publishers in order to access content (Waltham, 2003, p.8).

As an answer to these changes, the scholarly publishing has gradually become more services-oriented, supporting expectations of users in finding qualified information, and the required accessibility, search ability and navigability for scientific information. Thus, sophisticated services have been developed to enable searching across databases (Houghton et al., 2004, p.236), to make correlation between complementary information, to improve navigability through the content interconnecting subjects, documents, citations, authors or keywords, to deliver summaries, to give off-campus access, and to also make hyperlinks to referenced material, dynamic commentaries and social filtering .

The articles-based consumption of users requires the unbundling of journal components and the re-bundling in different, customised and customisable packages. On top of this, there is the low importance that journals brand can have to the new students and researchers generation, which will value articles, their authors and content more than the journal in which they were published. Houghton (2004, p.181) has pointed out that journal databases availability and the practice of searching by author or keywords have shown that users have been seeking for articles apart from the journal, evidencing that the journal itself has less importance to them.

Within this context, publishers will have to support the availability of high quality and carefully sorted information and digital services. However, firstly they need to know their customers' better. Waltham have emphasised that publishers should know users and interact with them in order to discover what they want and value and how they really use the online information. This will demand to keep closer to libraries and mainly, to make a substantial shift from publishers' product-centred focus to a more customer-centred perspective.

Impacts on business models : A financial perspective of business models was adopted in this study to outline the major impacts of e-publishing and to guide the subsequent analysis of some of these business models. The framework for e-business models which was proposed by Clarke (2004) was used to basis the analysis.

E- Books : Electronic books are also known as e-books. E-books are electronic version of books, delivered to readers in digital formats. They are read on all types of computers, including hand held devices designed specifically for reading e-books. Hence an electronic book should have electronic text and that text is to be represented to the reader visually. The electronic text is either saved to a floppy disk, transferred onto a CD-ROM, downloaded from the Internet or built into a palm-sized digital reader. There are a large number of devices being developed to make reading e-books easier for consumers. E-books can be as familiar as their print counterparts or as unique as the electronic medium itself, containing audio, video or live hyperlinks.

Special software, which makes documents or pages of a book easier to read on a screen, is also being developed by software companies. A standard for e-book software, known as the open e-book standard, or OEB, has been developed as a standard format for e-books, but competing standards such as Adobe's PDF exists. E-books can be delivered by download or e-mail attachments

Project Gutenberg of University of Illinois is one of the famous publisher of book length electronic texts, began in 1971. By the end of 2001, this publisher has created and distributed more than 10,000 electronic texts, which include several main categories of books including classics, light literatures and reference books.

Major Steps in Creation of E-books : E-books have definitely become the buzzword among authors and publishers. They are worried to create e-books which are inexpensive to produce, and can be updated or changed in a flash.

The first step of creation of e-book is to decide about the software product to be used to package the e-book. Right now the major choice of e-book publishers is Adobe Acrobat available on http://www.adobe.com. Acrobat makes an e-book perfectly formatted on the customers screen. In other words, if a word processor like Ms Word is used to format the book's layout, Acrobat would maintain the look of the file for the person reading. Acrobat-created documents are accessible to customers with both PCs and Macintosh computers. Most other programs do not provide this option. But it is important, as it allows serving the maximum number of buyers.

Another option is to create e-book as an HTML file, a language used for Web pages authoring. This method gives an opportunity to make e-book a multimedia production, with animation, audio, video. HyperMaker can produce executable .exe file after compiling all HTML files. Hyper Maker also enables e-book password protected, so that only a chapter or two is free. This way a potential buyer is allowed download a portion, copy, read a bit, and order immediate access if they want. The downfall to producing HTML e-books is that they are normally only readable to customers with PCs.

In the second step, the created e-book is to be made 'download ready'. This means that the e-book's file size should be smaller so that it downloads quickly onto the customer's computer. WinZip (http://www.winzip.com), is a popular compression program that makes this task very easy. This user-friendly software is very simple to use. It does every thing on behalf of the user once files to be compressed are selected. A file is created with an extension .zip (e.g., ebook.zip) to let user know that it's a zipped or shrunk file. Now as the e-book is zipped, there should be one way to decompress or unzip the file without WinZip. This means the zipped e-book file has to be transformed into a 'self-extracting' zip file. This facility is available with WinZip. In this way, even if the buyer does not have a zip program pre-installed on their system, the file will still open.

The third step is to upload the zipped e-book to the Web Server. It is same as uploading a web page to the Web server. Now the documents address would be the adding of the zipped file name after the website address. For example, the website address is http://www.ignou.ac.in and the e-book file name is ebook.zip, the complete download address would be http://www.ignou.ac.in/ebook.zip.

Reading Software and Hardware for E-books: E-books come in a variety of different flavours, for instance, certain e-books are read on handheld devices like the Rocket Book Reader <http://www.rocketbook.com>. Mega bookstore BarnesandNoble.com sells e-book tittles in this category. This software can be downloaded directly from the Internet onto the customer's computer. The customer then has the option of reading the e-book on screen, or printing it out.

The following file formats are used for e-books:

- DOC files are read with Microsoft Word or WordPad. DOC files are also compatible with the SoftBook Reader reading software and device.
- HTML files are read with Internet Browser software, which is pre-installed on most computers and available as a free download. HTML files are compatible with the Rocket eBook reading device.
- OeB is the Open eBook Standard format. SoftBook Reader and Microsoft Reader can read OeB compatible files. Rocket eBook is also compatible with OeB.
- PDF files are read with Adobe's Acrobat Reader or the Glassbook Reader, both available as a free download.

- RTF is considered the Universal file format because it works with any word processing program, PCs and Macs. WordPad or a word processing software package is needed to read .RTF files.
- TXT files are called Plain ASCII text. Any ASCII editor based on Windows or DOS may use to read them.
- WPD files are read with Corel's Word Perfect.

Hardware or reading devices are also important. The new generation of digital reading machines abandons the protocol that has defined the age of computing - scrolling - in favour of presenting text like a bound book; that is, it's a codex or sequence of pages. After years of punctuating the reading of every three or four paragraphs on a screen with a turning away of the eyes as the text rolls upward, there's a relief in simply clicking a button to get virtual page. The latest machines come with other refinements as well, such as electronic bookmarking, so one can automatically return to the page of last reading when the reader turns on again. The better quality machines also come with a built-in stylus, with reader annotation.

4.7.2. Electronic Journals

Electronic journal, e-journals in short, is a serial, produced, published and distributed in electronic media. Basically e-journal is one which is available in electronic form and can be accessed using computer and communication technologies. Often e-journals are called virtual journals, paperless journals, online journals, scholarly electronic journals, networked journals and CD-ROM journals, etc. Generally they are full text delivery systems and differ from conventional online bibliographic databases. All the activities of publishing from the initial stages of paper submission to publishing and distribution including accessing are performed using electronic media. With the emergence of Internet the prominence of e-journal is felt greatly. Electronic journal saves considerable time and effort on the part of authors, users and publishers.

4.7.3. Evolution of E-journals

The concept of e-journals was conceived with the full text databases offered by DIALOG in 1980. Dialog provided with only ASCII files of the journals, which stripped off the diagrams, photo, graphs from the text. With the advent of CDROM and allied technology it is possible to record and deliver full text of the journal as image file. During the year 1990 the online vendors started to deliver instantly the full text using CD-ROM and FAX. But they were unable to deliver any journals due to copyright issues. BHIL (Bell & Howell Information and Learning) successfully promoted this technology models for journals and offered LAN based solution with its image files of full text CD-ROM database of journals in the area of management, medical and social sciences. Later, ADONIS (Advanced Documents Over Network Information Systems) and IEEE followed the same LAN based models.

Major landmark in the world of e-journals is found with the advent of Internet. Many publishers are using the Web as a global way of offering their journals to international community. Of late, e-journals become the transformation of the Internet version available with different file format like HTML, SGML, PDF (Portable Document Format) image having facilities as a searchable file. During the last few years, scholarly electronic journals have been changed alot making a great impact among researchers and information professionals. In the 21st Century, publishing and citing e-journals are increased. For years publishers have been providing full-text access to a number of journals on CD-ROM, which requires a significant amount of hardware, time, and technical expertise on the subscriber's end. Libraries are experiencing declining trends in investment on acquisition of content. More so, declining trend is seen in investment on print versions. Spending for books has been particularly hard hit, while spending for online services and CD-ROM is showing a steady increase. Journal subscriptions have followed the same pattern, as well. Online and CD-ROM journals pose certain problems in terms of access. The scheme, in which electronic journals are made available to the subscribers, ensures that the powers of access and preservation remain in the hands of the publisher. Ease of accessing web prompts both publishers and scholars alike to put their contents on the web and the primary formats used are HTML, PDF, and increasingly, XML, and this has its own consequences for the professionals.

In under developed and developing countries its viability, with the existing infrastructure and pricing, has been viewed with great apprehension. Many ask whether e-publications are operated at much lower costs than print journals, and at the same time provide all the benefits of print journals. Lots of studies obviously come from developed countries but still do not provide a total and convincing solution to the problems expressed by readers and the library professionals. E-journals have almost all the characteristics of the print journals and would be available either online or offline or both.

4.7.4. Types of E-journals

Three types of electronic journals are available: i) online journals which are basically the online versions of the print journals; ii) CD-ROM journals which are full text journals published and distributed on CD-ROM media periodically and iii) networked electronic journals published and distributed via the Internet.

(a) Online journals : These journals are available on 'pay-as-you go' or 'cost-per access basis' via online hosts or vendors. Important online hosts providing online journals are

OCLC, Dialog, Bibliographic Retrieval Services (BRS), STN International, etc. Due to high cost and limited access of the users to remote online systems, online journals are not generally considered as a part of the library collection. Electronic versions of some of the existing printed journals are also available. For example the journals of the American Chemical Society are available online through the STN International.

(b) CD-ROM Journals : These are full text journals published and distributed in the form of CD-ROM at a different frequency along with a search software to access and print. Mostly they are the electronic versions of existing print journals. Numbers of publishers (both commercial and learned society) have started publishing some of their core journals in CD-ROM form. Important examples are the journals and conference proceedings of IEEE, ABI-INFORM, a full text business periodical published by University Microfilm International and ADONIS published by Elsevier Publishers.

(c) Networked e-journals : These are the electronic versions of existing journals or only electronic version available over the network either on or any other commercial smaller networks. Internet has enabled the publishing task much easier and faster. Many printed journals are available in electronic form over Internet either free of charge or on subscription. Many journals have no print versions and are available only on the Net. The number of e-journals available on Internet increases rapidly by time. They are based on mailing listsoftware or client/server computing applications including www. These can be newsletters, discussion lists, un-moderated bulletin boards, peer reviewed journals and popular magazines. The networked e-journals can be distributed by the following ways:

(i) *Contents page and abstracts* : The central computer holds a list of subscribers and sends them contents page and abstracts of articles by e-mail of the newly published issues. The subscribers can retrieve the relevant articles through file transfer protocol (FTP) or GET command using e-mail itself so that the articles are delivered to their e-mail boxes.

(ii) *Full text delivery*: Subscribers are automatically sent the full text of each newly published issue by e-mail.

(iii) *Client/server technology* : Numbers of e-journals are now being published with the application of client/ server technology. For example e-journals can be accessed via Gopher, where a desktop gopher client connects to a gopher server and via www where a desktop client such as Mosaic, Netscape connects to web servers. The method has been found to be very useful for accessing e-journals in recent years.

Of all types, network e-journals are most popular and easily accessible. They are used almost synonymously to e-journals. Now-a-days, an e-journal is referred generally to a networked e-journal. There are three access models to e-journals

(a) **Remote Access**: Publishers host their journals at their website. Access Permission is provided, when the library or individual subscribes to the e-journals. Publishers offer the rights through one of the following methods

(i) *User ID and Password*: the subscriber gets a user id and password, which can be used from any user terminal in the library. This is suitable for dial up access users.

(ii) Have intranet based LAN in their libraries or campus. Here publisher's server site will recognize and validate the IP address of subscriber's intranet server when each time a user logs into publisher's website for a subscribed journal

(iii) *Combined*: both of the aforesaid access methods are also offered by the publishers.

(b) On Site Access : Publishers deliver the e-journals to subscribers through CD-ROM or through their website or FTP option. This is more suitable than above methods because it is more secure to maintain the journal at its end as it has paid for the journal (the library) and is used to the ownership concept. As library can host the journal within its campus through LAN it offers wider and better bandwidth for access than access through Internet.

(c) Access through Database : The access and use of information in an electronic/digital format is not a new concept. Some publishers have been producing their content in an electronic format for years. Access models offered by publishers limit the access to their journals, but the users often find articles of their interest through database.

The bibliographic databases have emerged as user's favourite/preferred interface for searching and locating information. Seamless access to information is achieved through the link model offered by database producers and vendors.

4.7.5. Advantages of E-journals

With the emergence of Internet, the publication of e-journals has the following advantages for both libraries as well as to the user community.

(i) The speed of publication and delivery of the journal issues is much faster than the print versions.

(ii) Inclusion of audio and video base text in the journal issues is possible.

(iii) To access and retrieve relevant articles, a good number of search engines are available.

(iv) Downloading and printing of relevant articles at the end user workstations is possible.

(v) E-journals have solved many problems of libraries such as space, shelving, missing issues, missing pages and cutting of the pages, etc.

(vi) Multiple access and access through local networks becomes easy.

(vii) Provide hyperlinks, i.e., links to the related articles cited in each article and other useful sources.

(viii) Help in minimizing the problems related to the conservation and preservation of journals.

(ix) Cost of publication and distribution is less than the print versions.

(x) Alerting the users regarding the publication of new issues and articles of their interest becomes easier in electronic media.

4.7.6. Limitations of E-journals

With the increasing popularity of the e-journals, its publication has come across with many limitations which are to be considered. Due to the emergence of Internet the following factors cum constrains concerning the usage of e-journals are to be taken care.

(i) No Ownership : The subscriber, whether it's a library or an individual, becomes the owner of a printed journal which is not possible in case of e-journals. So the concepts like 'library has' or 'library has not' is no more in existence for e-journals. A major shift in case of e-journal is concerned not with owning it but having permission to access it. Most of the publishers of e-journals maintain a limited period (say one year) for accessing them, and accessing beyond that period means paying extra charges. The library or the user has to pay for accessing the journals rather than owning them.

(ii) Infrastructure : The subscribers of the e-journals require the necessary computer with Internet facilities to access, download and preserve them which may not be possible for all the libraries or users. Cost involved in creating the entire infrastructure, network connection and printing may be deferent in using e-journals.

(iii) Archiving: Till today many libraries are not updated with new technological applications. In fact many of them find it difficult to cope with the technology. E-journals, especially issues for several years with back runs require large disk space to store and archive, and some libraries have limitations in this respect. Even if the data are stored, retrieving, providing printouts on demand, upgrading the retrieval software, etc. are some of the problems that the libraries encounter.

(iv) Standardization: Production of e-journals generally lack clear-cut standardization regarding its format and the software associated in accessing them. E-journals users should be acquainted with the technical know-how associated with them, which is not possible in all cases. Some of the e-journals do not include page numbers as the size of the page varies according to the display area of different computer (except pdf file). This raises citation problem when the same material to be cited can appear in different pages. This necessitates training of library staff and users which creates problems to the library and takes considerable time and effort.

(v) Acceptability: In spite of tremendous technological innovations and their applications to digitized information, many people are strongly in favour of paper media. Hence, librarians, authors and users are yet to accept e-journals as viable alternative to print versions. Perhaps it will take some more time for the users of e-journals to realize the full advantages of e-journals.

(vi) Mode of Subscription : For print media journals, they are selected based on certain procedures like asking for quotations, sample issues and evaluation, etc. by the libraries before they are being procured. Some e-journal publishers offer free trial subscription for a period. The procedures for procuring e-journals are to be changed or modified accordingly to make them suitable. Even for browsing an e-journal the user has to pay for it which the user may not always like to do. A well-accepted method of subscription has not yet been achieved.

(vii) Scrolling: Computers cannot display a full page at a time and need scrolling of the screen for browsing which is very uncomfortable for a reader. It is not possible to browse through a digital document without accessing it.

(viii) Bibliographic control : No suitable bibliographic control mechanism is available for e-journals. It becomes difficult for a user to identify a particular e-journal or even to be aware of the publication of e-journals over the network.

Despite several problems, the e-journals are very popular particularly because of the possibility of the multimedia and hypermedia linkages among the electronic resources which is not possible in print versions. The librarians should be prepared to handle them to make them easily accessible to the users.

4.8. DTP SOFTWARE

Desktop publishing software can turn copy and media files into publishable layouts, for things such as newspapers, magazines, brochures, flyers, and books. Completed layouts can be uploaded onto a website or exported and printed onto paper or similar materials. Users can use prepackaged templates or build pages from scratch, and edit individual pages to meet the needs of each projects. Desktop publishing tools may integrate with drawing or photo editing tools, and are commonly used by the editorial and layout staff within an organization. Completed layouts can be uploaded onto a website or exported and printed onto paper or similar materials.

Desktop publishing (DTP) is the creation of documents using page layout software on a personal ("desktop") computer. It was first used almost exclusively for print publications, but now it also assists in the creation of various forms of online content Desktop publishing software can generate layouts and produce typographic-quality text and images comparable to traditional typography and printing. Desktop publishing is also the main reference for digital typography. This technology allows individuals, businesses, and other organizations to self-publish a wide variety of content, from menus to magazines to books, without the expense of commercial printing.

Desktop publishing often requires the use of a personal computer and WYSIWYG page layout software to create documents for either large-scale publishing or small-scale local multifunction peripheral output and distribution – although a non-WYSIWYG system such as LaTeX could also be used for the creation of highly structured and technically demanding documents as well. Desktop publishing methods provide more control over design, layout, and typography than word processing. However, word processing software has evolved to include most, if not all, capabilities previously available only with professional printing or desktop publishing.

The same DTP skills and software used for common paper and book publishing are sometimes used to create graphics for point of sale displays, presentations, infographics, brochures, business cards, promotional items, trade show exhibits, retail package designs and outdoor signs. Although what is classified as "DTP software" is usually limited to print and PDF publications, DTP isn't limited to print. The content produced by desktop publishers may also be exported and used for electronic media. The job descriptions that include "DTP," such as DTP artist, often require skills using software for producing e-books, web content, and web pages, which may involve web design or user interface design for any graphical user interface.

Desktop publishing tools allow users to create and publish page designs and printable materials in a polished, professional style. Digital creations comprise text and graphics and can be made for print and online viewing. Additionally, materials can be exported in a variety of different formats.

Desktop publishing tools often come with premade templates that require little to no editing, so the software is ideal for inexperienced users. For expert designers and experienced users, the tool also comes with many editing and design features that facilitate the creation of custom layouts for specific use cases.

4.8.1. Key Benefits of Desktop Publishing Software

- Provides prebuilt templates for page designs
- Let's users edit and design page layouts
- Allows users to export and share high-quality designs in a variety of formats

Why Use Desktop Publishing Software? Desktop publishing software is ideal for all types of businesses that create and publish distributed content, whether it's internal or consumer-facing.

Flyers : Flyers are typically created for advertising purposes. They are one-page handouts that are often colorful and designed to be eye-catching. Marketing and advertising teams can use desktop publishing software to design flyers for distribution.

Newsletters : Newsletters are bulletin-style prints that are created to showcase news, events, and other notable activities related to the distributor. Desktop publishing software makes it easy for businesses to create memorable newsletters for internal or client-facing updates.

Articles : Articles typically have specific layouts that include columns and unique line spacing. Desktop publishing software often comes with prebuilt article templates to make creating these specific layouts easier for businesses.

Posters : Desktop publishing software also includes ways to create engaging posters for larger designs. Despite the size, desktop publishing tools ensure image quality is retained throughout the printing process.

Who Uses Desktop Publishing Software? The approachable design features of desktop publishing software makes it easy for any business to implement without much training beyond the commonly included platform tutorials. Writers, designers, and marketers commonly use desktop publishing software for creating and distributing published materials.

Writers : Newsletters, articles, blogs, and other published content can be easily created using desktop publishing software. Writers and editors can write within the platform and design the layout using prebuilt templates or their own design.

Designers : Designers can use desktop publishing software to create and edit new and existing page layouts for businesses. For example, a business may request a custom newsletter template for internal distribution. Designers can create a template for businesses and export it into an editable format for that business. Additionally, designers can also design article templates for writers and editors.

Marketers : Marketers typically benefit from the poster and flyer design capabilities of desktop publishing software. This tool comes with templates and stock image repositories for efficient material creation.

4.8.2. Desktop Publishing Software Features

Desktop publishing tools come with a wide variety of design-focused features that are straightforward and easy to use. Additionally, these tools also offer supplementary features that help users share and export their designed materials.

Layout editor : The overall layout editor encompasses a variety of design capabilities, including editing images, text, borders, and more.

Prebuilt templates : Prebuilt templates come with fully formed material designs and are organized by material type.

Prebuilt newsletters, articles, and other types of materials can be chosen and edited further by the user.

Publishing formats : Created designs can be easily exported and shared within the desktop publishing platform. In addition to the digital exporting features, designs can also be optimized for printing. Print optimization takes size into account to ensure the designs retain their quality during the printing process.

Layout adaptation : Layout adaptation automatically formats images and content to fit perfectly into blank areas of available space. For example, a column within a newsletter that has an area suited for an image will automatically scale the image to fit the area, so the user does not have to spend time resizing the image.

Saved preferences : For designers who often work with a specific layout, desktop publishing software can save specific preferences, such as the template and export type, automatically. This lets the designer create and distribute the layout multiple times without starting from scratch.

Potential Issues with Desktop Publishing Software

Printing issues : Digital materials have more robust color availability compared to printed materials. Most ink printers are only capable of using the RGB color mode (red, green, and blue). In some cases, ink colors can be expanded, but it still would not compare to the vast color schemes available digitally. Laser printers can be used in place of ink printers to print particularly colorful materials, but they are often expensive.

4.8.3. Software and Services Related to Desktop Publishing Software

Vector graphics software and photo editing software both complement desktop publishing tools well:

Vector graphics software : Vector graphics software is used to create vector images and illustrations, which can be easily exported into desktop publishing software to be used in materials created within the platform.

Photo editing software : For more robust photo editing capabilities, users can use photo editing software to enhance images that can be later exported into desktop publishing software.

4.9. SUMMARY

The Emerging Technology in e- publishing is expected to bring about significant improvements over current modes of electronic publishing and access methods of the information. The library professionals, Educators, researchers and students across the world will be among the first to benefit from electronic publishing particularly those in the developing countries in the electronic era. In this changing scenario, Electronic Publishing provides a number of benefits not only to the librarian but also to the facilitators, instructors, gatekeepers of knowledge interpreters, evaluators, consultants, researchers, information managers, promoters, editors, content creators, publishes and archives. Therefore, the utilization of electronic publishing is rapidly growing within the technical community.

4.10. REVIEW QUESTIONS

1. Describe E-journals and e-books?
2. What is DTP software?
3. List the type of E-journals?

Unit 5

OBJECTIVES

- To learn about Electronic Resources
- To know about e-publishing
- To share use and usability of e-publishing

5.1. INTRODUCTION

Technology forms one of the key enables for the implementation of knowledge, services and applications. Many of the commonly available approaches to knowledge would be rendered in effective in the absence of technology. The innovation and knowledge creation emphasis the creation of new knowledge through basic and applied research development. E-publishing is helpful in producing documents containing texts, graphics, still or motion pictures, audio, tables, numeric, equations, etc. all of these will the assistance at a data processing system. It may involve the products and services which may be distributed and used without ever appearing in printed form. It may be carried out as a primary commercial concern (eg. Newspapers, Books, Magazines) or as a vital components of other organized process such as administration, research, education. At present the World Wide Web provides the most visible and fast expanding environment for these activities. Electronic information handling is a broad and flexible concept with plenty of degrees of freedom, adapted to the fluid and living nature of today's information material. It encompasses data collection, analysis, dissemination, and so on, as well as publishing. The emergence of the electronic medium is currently best represented by the World Wide Web. The WWW is based on hyper text and hyper media. The explosion of electronic documents is however without bringing is new questions, new challenges and new problems that will have to be faced especially on the ethical, legal and educational levels, without forgetting the security nor the fragility of the material delivered on the electronic medium. It must be clear that, wishing to maintain at all costs compatibility between post scripts, PDF and HTML (something that is repeatedly in publishing ventures) would prevent taking advantage of the hyper textual structure, sound, motion, applets and whatever may come next, available on the electronic medium.

The proliferation of E-publishing across the world has brought in a revolution in scholarly journal publication, subscription, and access and delivery mechanism. E-journals are electronic equivalents of their print counter parts possessing many added features. E-journals offer a range of potential advantages to libraries and end-users: multiple simultaneous access to the same issue, remote access, in-built searching facilities, multi-media capabilities and reduced storage concerns. As a result of the above, libraries today buy licenses for an ever-increasing number of E-Journals from a range of different publishers and providers. At the same time the library budgets are dwindling and hence librarians are forced to work together for alternate strategies towards collection enrichment and sharing of resources. Consortium based library subscriptions to E-journals and electronic full-text Databases are picking up good momentum in India. Over the past five years more than ten national level

The number of academic eBooks in university libraries is increasing. Reading digital materials such as newspapers is valued in India; however, students' perceptions of the value of reading academic e-Materials are not well known. The experiences from the students generally affirmed that the technology has potential to enhance teaching and learning in a university setting. However, the experiences (especially of the long-term users) highlight a number of challenges that need to be addressed.

5.2. ELECTRONIC RESOURCES

Electronic resources delivers the collection of information as full text databases, e-journals, image collections, multimedia in the form of CD, tap, internet, web technology etc. It is a computer aided or assisted process of publishing in which the documents are submitted in electronic form. Scientists describe it is an application of Information Technology to traditional print publishing and according to them the term electronic publishing refers more precisely to the storage and retrieval of digitized information through electronic communication media. So e-publishing can be represented I, e, e-publishing= information technology (computer technology =communication technology) + publishing technology.

5.2.1. Evolution of electronic publishing

Among the major contributions of the industrial era, outstanding are the evolution and growth of information publishing and printing facilities that use tools to record, store and distribute information. In the last ten years, the first step was taken toward the storage and reproduction of sounds and images in new multimedia formats. Technological advances also have brought new possibilities in accessing and disseminating information. Electronic publishing has been particularly effective in accelerating access and contributing to the generation of additional knowledge, consequently, an exponential increase in data has taken place, most notably in the second half of the twentieth century. The access to electronic scientific publications via internet is providing to be an alternative for maintaining these collections at lower cost. It also provides greater ability in publishing and distributing the periodical, and in the final users accessing of the information. During the last few years the e-publishing industry has spread over with increasing complexities and emergence of other concept in to it. UNESCO, as early as in 1996, started that "the development of new carriers for the storage of information, traditionally produced on paper, has brought about fundamental change in thinking within national libraries about future collection policies and storage requirements. The concept of e-publishing covers a variety of publishing models and formats.

E-publishing models include commercial e-publishing, subsidy e-publishing, distributors, and self e-publishing.

Vanity epublishing is sometimes called as a subsidy publishing since the author pays a subsidy to get a book published. Subsidy e-publishers, like their print counterparts, produce and distribute book for a certain fee per manuscript. Authors receive a royalty, which is usually comparable to that offered by commercial e-publishers. Electronic self-publishing is a process in which the author is entirely responsible for producing his own book, form development to publication to marketing.

5.3. ACCESS OF E-RESOURCES

The electronic resources can be accessed by the respondents at different places such as Home, Department and Library etc. It is essential to know the favourite place of access of e-resources by the respondents form each departments. Electronic Journal is a serial, produced, published and distributed in electronic media. Basically e-journal is one which is available in electronic form and can be accessed using computer and communication technology. Often e-journals are called virtual journals, paperless journals, online journals, scholarly electronic journals, networked journals, and CDROM journals, etc.

5.3.1. Collection Development

The term 'collection' in the phrases is seems not sufficient today. Collections and connections are likely to be winning as a better replacement to address today's complex premise of electronic media with online dissemination of information. Since the application of Information Technology in publishing, the world seems to have exploded with digital products and its remote distribution. Different modes of electronic publishing are concurrently operational in the current market.

Digital Learning: Education in cloud- It is possible that by the year 2020, no student would have to go to school or college. The entire curriculum might be available on the cloud, which student might be able to access from the comfort of their home or even the playground. We expect broadband connectivity to become widely available by 2020.

E-space for learning : Online learning (e-learning):- A web- based learning mechanism could be used within the institution or outside it. It needs to consider aspects such as flexibility, modularization, assistance form experts, interactivity, instantaneous access to course and reference materials.

Findings : The Internet has provided writers a new way to reach vast audiences and promote publishing e-books. This has much greater impact on the book business than technological advances in publisher workflow, low cost, easy production, reviving out-of-print. The e-publishing helps in storing the manuscript as an electronic file until a customer places an order.

5.4. USABILITY OF DIGITAL LIBRARIES

Digital libaries can be evaluated on three key components, viz. contents, functionality and user interface (Van House et al, 1996). A number of studies have taken place in the recent past on the usability of digital libraries. The HCI community always emphasizes on the usability of the user interfaces. For them usability testing involves assessing the effectiveness, efficiency and/ or satisfaction of the user with a particular interface (Choudhury, Hobbs and Lorie, 2002; Nielsen, 1993; Norlin, 2000). Bollen and Luce (2002) comment that some usability factors such as user preferences and satisfaction tend to be highly transient and specific, and therefore research on these issues need to focus on more stable characteristics of a given user community, such as 'the community's perspective on general document impact and the realtionships between documents in a collection.' Park (2000) comments that most earlier studies on the usability of multiple online databases have focussed on technical and performance issues rather than interaction issues. Park's study shows that users prefer to interact with multiple databases through a common interfaces rather than an integrated interface because the former provides more control for the users on the selection of databases. Cultural issues have significant influence on the usability of digital libraries. Emphasizing the importance of cultural issues on the usability of information services, Duncker, Theng and Mohd-Nasir (2000) comment that misinterpretation of the importance of colours, forms, symbols, metaphors, language and use for users coming from different cultural backgrounds can significantly affect the usability and user friendliness of digital libraries. 5 Bishop et al (2000) comments that 'users don't know what they don't know, don't understand what they don't understand, and in any case, don't want to talk about it in a survey.' Hence researchers should be careful in choosing the method for studying the usability of digital librries involving end users. Recent studies on usability testing with specific references to digital libraries include those of Blanford and Buchanan (2003), Allen (2002), Dickstein and Mills (2000), and Mitchell (1999). Usability issues of e-books have been widely studied and reported on by Landoni and her associates (see for example, Wilson and Landoni,2003; Wilson, Landoni and Gibb, 2003; and Wilson, Shortreed and Landoni, 2004)

5.5. ECONOMICS OF E- PUBLISHING

The economics of electronic publishing I will concentrate upon the equivalent of the typical academic book – what we have come to refer to as the long linear document. In what follows, lacking a good brief term for this, I will speak of 'documents'. Although it is the long linear document that is in the forefront of my mind, most of what I will say would apply equally to documents with hypertext and/or multimedia components. And in some parts of the argument those kinds of document display the characteristics about which I am speaking more acutely than do simple documents.

We can start from several directions but I want to focus on the most important element in the process — the reader. We must be careful not to allow either the economics or the technology to distract us from the fundamental purpose of the whole endeavor. The point is not words on a screen or type on a page, but ideas in a mind.

So let us focus on the academic reader. The essential characteristics of academic readers are that they are expert and time constrained. As experts they want to make their own choices of what to read, but being time constrained they wish to make their choices of what to read with least time consumed in the selection process, the least time spent reading things that are not valuable, and they want the actual reading process to be efficient and effective.

An academic reader also wants to know about all the important strands of thinking in her discipline, and wants to stay in touch with work in other fields that have relevance to her work. This last consideration is of increasing significance in the fluid world of present day humanities and social sciences. This may be one major factor differentiating the reading patterns of scholars in the humanities and certain social sciences from reading patterns in the sciences.

A century or so ago most of these were not issues. The intelligent lay person could keep abreast of a wide sweep of human knowledge. Now an academic, even with a light teaching load, struggles to keep in touch with all that is written which is of immediate relevance to her work. And no one expects the pace of new writing to slow. Indeed many predictions suggest that the availability of electronic channels for dissemination will have a liberating effect on the productivity of scholars. That is to say, that the easy availability of electronic channels will make more documents available.

Faced with a scarce resource — in this case time to read — an economist argues that the scarce resource has a real value and that misuse of that valuable resource has a real cost. We may not go through a careful process of assigning a dollar value to it, but we should nonetheless aim to use it as parsimoniously as we spend money. In a profession such as the law where the meter is always running, no one has any difficulty in understanding this. When we look inside the academy, this point is much less widely appreciated. No doubt one explanation is that academics usually love their work and thus draw a much looser boundary between work and leisure than do most people. But their days still only have 24 hours like everyone else's — time constrained means time has a value.

So when we think about an academic reader, we are dealing with a resource — her time — with a real economic value. And that fact must guide our exploration of the way a manuscript, via whatever delivery mechanism, should go from its author to its reader.

5.6. THE INFORMATION INTERMEDIARY

In a simple and small world, all authors and readers would have direct contact and documents would move directly from creator to reader. Readers would know authors and their work and decide on the basis of that direct knowledge whether a work was worth their time to read. As the size of the population increases, and as it becomes more dispersed and less homogeneous, that direct method breaks down and a need develops for some intermediation between author and reader.

There may well be disciplines, or at least subfields, where the direct communication model still applies. One can sketch certain necessary characteristics of such a field: small size, relatively low output per scholar, general agreement about the scope of the discipline, and general agreement about quality.

While complete fields of this kind may be rare, there are many disciplines where much of the elite communicates informally through working papers — a form of dissemination that is not intermediated. What is concerning there is the exclusionary consequence. Those not connected to the elite networks tend to be left behind and left voiceless. As we consider the need for intermediaries and their role, broadening access both to readers and authors should be a serious consideration. This is of course a challenge as the selectivity necessary for other reasons can conflict with such democracy.

What are the tasks of these intermediaries? I identify four: gathering, selecting, enhancing, and informing. There are of course at present two main kinds of knowledge intermediary: the library and the publisher, and each of the four tasks has a somewhat different meaning for each intermediary. But one important publisher activity fits outside this schema and deserves a brief mention. Book editors, but also some journal editors, persuade scholars to write works which they believe are needed and would be valuable. In many cases also, the publisher works to persuade a scholar that her work is worth synthesizing into a book-length document. I am not going to explore this activity further, but raise it here not only for completeness but also to make clear that the range of material to be gathered in and selected from is not exogenous – it is not purely a given - the intermediaries create and influence what is written in a wide variety of ways.

In the paper world, the four tasks as done by the publisher primarily precede the four tasks performed by the library. This is something of a simplification of the library's full range of work, but it does apply over a wide range of library activities.

Gathering : The publisher gathers in the writings of authors both reactively and proactively. The existence of a large number of publishers permits them to gather writings from a wide range of sources and to provide a quite comprehensive service which saves scholars from having to seek out the works for themselves. This saves scholars' time and of course makes possible a much wider catchment area (literally and metaphorically) than any one individual could monitor. Now it may be that in an electronic publishing world, the task of gathering will be eliminated, although I would not expect the facility for seamless worldwide searching to be practical and available to all for some considerable time. There seems likely to continue to be a need for some kind of knowledge intermediary hunting and gathering across the net.

Selection : I choose the word 'selection' rather than 'gatekeeping' because 'gatekeeping' has a passive connotation: it conjures a vision of a flow of people autonomously arriving at a gate and being considered for entry. St. Peter may be assured of a reliable flow of candidates, the publisher feels a definite need to seek them out.

As a publisher considers a new work or proposal, two sets of criteria are applied so that two types of signals can be sent to readers to guide their later reading choices. The first kind of signal is a pure quality one: this work is worth your time to read. The more discriminating the publisher, the more the scholar can trust the signal. And of course that trust goes back not just to the publisher but to the academics who as advisors and editorial board members steer the editorial decisions of university presses. The second kind of signal is about the kind of work. Most good publishers have an editorial policy: they endeavor to select works of a particular kind even within a discipline. The scholar with certain interests and tastes can therefore know whether what that publisher offers is likely to be appeal. Thus in two ways the publisher's selection process reduces time costs for the reader.

Before I go on, it is time to point out that what I am talking about is value added. I have avoided the term so far, but the time that is saved for the academic reader is a value added service to the reader. Indeed I would posit time saved as one important way of defining and quantifying value added. And of course an entirely media neutral measure.

Enhancement : The third task of the intermediary between author and reader is enhancement. Under this term I include everything that is done to the author's work which changes it before it reaches the reader. This is probably the area where the electronic world will in due course look very different from the present paper world. However amongst the functions that will in some form carry over are editing (revise and resubmit is surely media independent), copyediting, or some components at least of that activity, and design — the formatting of material to make it easy to read, easy to navigate around, and generally to make it an effective device for conveying the message of the document. As we redefine this general task of document enhancement — whether it be traditional style copyediting, the provision of hypertextual links or integration of multi-media, the dominant question will have to be about the relationship between cost incurred and value added.

Informing : Finally there is the task of informing potential readers — what is vulgarly called marketing. Some believe retrieval tools will make this unnecessary. Considering the complex interest matrices in the humanities, I suspect that many scholars will continue to welcome a contribution to the process by active knowledge purveyors and will not want to rely completely on the passive knowledge/active seeker model which is so often implicit in predictions of the future. That the methods and mechanisms employed will change, indeed are changing, is undeniable.

Library Value Added: Turning now to the definition of these tasks for the library, I must be much more cautious given my lack of relevant expertise. So a few brief comments. First, although payment for value added is interestingly absent from most of the library world, clearly we must think of the library tasks within the same framework of benefits, especially time saving benefits, for scholars. While the publisher gathers and then selects from the manuscript universe, the library has traditionally selected from the universe of publications: works that have survived the publisher selection process.

We might ask the rationale for this two-stage process. There are I think two reasons. First the publishers provide a multitude of entry channels and thus ensure there is no monopoly of ideas. But second there are considerable economies of scale in the selection process: one publisher discriminates for many (indeed all) libraries. The economies of scale argument is reinforced by the decisions of most libraries to use vendor systems to reduce to manageable proportions the number of publications from which they have to choose. The vendor rather than the library gathers and does a partial selection.

At the library level, enhancement is very different. It tends to be a matter of multi-document organization rather than single document enhancement — although we might well see some library intervention in the organization and presentation of documents once they are in electronic form and thus transformable.

The function of informing is illuminatingly different. Although libraries do disseminate some information about what has become available to their user community, the special expertise is the reverse of the publisher's: the active-searcher passive-information mode: the skilled searching for what the reader needs. I have increasingly come to feel that this distinction between the direction of activity along the knowledge conduit is important to re-envisioning the roles of publishers and librarians in the future.

Measuring value added

Having identified a range of ways value is added by the intermediators between author and reader, we need to think about the process by which that value added is reflected in revenue received by the body adding value. And here we come upon an interesting difference: the publisher as intermediary has primarily expected that his efforts at adding value will be recognized by readers paying for those efforts. On the other hand, the library has generally expected that the community, be it college, city or club, will pay for its efforts because of some perceived general utility of the value that it adds. No one seems to believe that the library's level and range of services should be defined by market criteria – what it can sell for a sufficient amount to pay its costs. But the contrary presumption is usually made of university presses.

For the moment I will leave that observation to stand but will return to it later. It does though, I hope, raise questions in all your minds as to whether making decisions based purely on market criteria is wise for intellectual and culturally important services and goods. Subsidization of music and theater by both government and private donors certainly suggests a pervasive belief (but sadly not universal) that some things are too central to our culture to be left to the Darwinian struggle of the market place.

5.7. INADEQUACY OF MARKET SIGNALS

There are in fact good economic arguments for recognizing that market signals will not always be the appropriate ones for determining what is provided. And I want briefly to present three economic reasons why books and even more so electronic documents fall into the category of goods whose provision should not be solely decided by the market.

Cultural concerns : First, imagine that a university library charged a serious amount for use of its holdings; and decided what it would add to those holdings based on the revenue generated from various sections. With substantial research grants, the scientists would probably be little deterred by charges for use. Indeed even large access charges would hardly be significant relative to their equipment costs, for example. On the other hand, humanities scholars, usually without research money, would be strongly deterred from library use. The consequence would be a marked decrease in the purchase of new humanities works in the library and a shift of yet more resources to science and technology holdings. I am sure that none of us would welcome that. I hope it raises questions about the use of a market mechanism of this kind to guide library collection development.

But there are more fundamental reasons why the market should not be relied upon to generate best solutions in our areas of concern.

Public Goods : Books and even more electronic documents possess tow of the characteristics of what economists call public goods. It is a basic theorem of economics that the market under-provides public goods. That is to say, if the market is relied upon to determine the supply of a public good, the amount produced and sold will be less than the amount that maximizes society's welfare. Too few resources will go into producing public goods and too many into producing conventional private goods — apples, shirts and handguns.

The two characteristics that imbue documents with publicans are non-exhaustibility and non-excludability.

Non-Exhaustibility : The first of these is based on the non-exhaustibility of the document in either paper or electronic form. One person consumes an apple — it is gone. One person reads a book and it is unchanged, ready to be used again. Something of course that even more true of an electronic file. The economic theory that underpins blind faith in market solutions specifically does not apply to goods that are not used up in the act of consumption. Indeed economic theory shows that such goods will be under-provided relative to simple economic goods, and that non-market devices are needed if society is to have the right amount of such goods. Museums, rural roads, public health endeavors all come under this category.

Non-Excludability : The second reason is based on the non-excludability of documents. In a paper world, the existence of photocopying means that some readers obtain a document not from the publisher but by making a copy of the original publication. They thus gain value from the document but contribute nothing to the publisher to recompense for the costs incurred in creating that value added. The result of this is that some documents are not published which would not only generate value added for readers, but whose total value added would be greater than the costs of making the work available. Society is therefore less well-off than it would have been had the publisher not had to assume that his revenue would reflect only a part of the value added. It seems nearly gratuitous to remark that this phenomenon threatens to be much more serious in an electronic publishing world with the extraordinary ease and cheapness of copying a file.

Declining Costs : There is another quite separate argument that market based solutions lead to under-provision of books (and again a fortiori electronic documents). This is based on the distinctive cost structure of books, a structure that journals share and so, in a more extreme form, do electronic documents. The essential fact is that most publishing costs are incurred in getting to the point where we can make the first copy, or send the first copy over the net. And the costs of making additional copies are small (in electronic publishing - probably very close to zero). Economic theory argues that output of a good should be expanded until the cost of the last copy made is equal to the benefit to the last buyer who buys the last item sold. If we stop before that point, there are buyers who would gain utility greater than the social cost of making that item who do not in fact obtain it.

Society's net benefit is maximized if the price of obtaining the document should equal the incremental cost of producing the document. But that means that sales revenue or user fees or whatever is not available to cover the first copy costs. Thus consider an example:

first copy costs	$5,000
incremental cost is $3 cost of 1000 copies	$3,000
total expenses	$8,000
revenue from 1000 copies sold at price=incremental cost	$3,000
Publisher's loss	$5,000

So there is a clear and substantial conflict between the publisher's need to cover costs and the optimum of having price equal to incremental cost. And with the incremental cost in the electronic environment close to zero, the situation is more acute than the example I have just presented.

There is nothing new about this situtation. Academic publishers have always had to price well above incremental cost. So buyers who would gain benefit from possession of the book that is greater than society's cost of providing the book have been deterred from purchase. Various mechanisms for recovering some of the first copy costs without loading them onto the individual purchaser have developed. Subsidies and help in kind to university presses, title specific subsidies e.g. from the NEH; subsidies e.g. from Getty to support exceptionally high first copy costs. Also higher prices to libraries than to individuals, either through differential subscriptions or though different editions – paper for the individual, cloth for the library, operate to bring the individual purchase price closer to incremental cost. Interestingly the library can be seen contributing to this end in another way: rather than subsidizing the producer to bring price down to marginal cost, society has preferred a mechanism that subsidizes the consumer by permitting free use but not ownership of books.

5.8. COST RECOVERY SOLUTIONS

Solutions in which optimal pricing and cost recovery are not in harmony are quite common. There are three types of solutions: socialization, special tariffs, mutualization. I will talk briefly about each as each does raise issues of some significance.

Socialization : It is very common to provide such goods through a government agency. Roads are a good example: huge first user costs, trivial or zero costs per user in non-congested situations. They are naturally provided and supported from ppublic funds. So should we just nationalize the provision of academic writings, or set up some organization jointly armed by all universities? I doubt any of us find these options especially attractive. But raising the topic points to a very important issue in any re-design of our existing system — the need for diverse and independent channels.

It is easy when focusing on economic solutions to lose sight of the crucial importance of our topic: at root we are talking of the exchange of ideas — and the free exchange of ideas. We cannot afford to invent solutions that do anything to endanger the freedom of individuals to express ideas conformist and maverick, radical or traditional. The great strength of our present system is the variety of places to which an author can turn to get his or her work published. This we must preserve.

The university presses have evolved into organizations that do provide this freedom. There are a substantial number, over 100 members of the AAUP, each formulating a distinct editorial policy. Their editorial decisions are made in collaboration between press editors and a faculty committee — university administrators rarely have any say in what is published. In my experience faculty boards are very aware if their responsibility to provide a channel for a wide variety of ideas and defend that freedom jealously.

In addition, university presses have been energetic in supporting emergent fields. The fact that sales do matter in their operations means sensitivity to new trends and developments in the academy. And the number and variety of presses is a good insurance that routes to publication will be available for those fields and those scholars struggling to put forward new perspectives.

Thus in this consideration of institutional designs, I want to reject monolithic solutions to the cost recovery problem. But more — the provision of diverse routes to publication must be a very central criterion in evaluating any proposed changes.

Special tariffs : The second type of solution to the cost recovery problem is special pricing structures. There is an enormous literature and a very technical one on designing pricing schemes for industries with cost characteristics like those of publishing. Much of this literature is driven by the problems of pricing for electric utilities that are faced with very much the same problem as we are.

This problem can be expressed: we need to recover high initial costs while setting a price close to incremental cost so that no one whose benefit from the product is greater than the incremental cost will be deterred from buying.

One common structure for this kind of problem is what has recently been described to me as country club pricing. You pay a membership fee but then pay incremental costs for all the things you do within the country club. There are many other similar applications of this kind of system. Gregory Rawlings proposal is of this kind. We might envision a journal charging a subscription fee which buys you the right not to receive a traditional journal but to have copies of articles you want sent to you at whatever the incremental cost of sending might be.

However all applications have one thing in common. The customer is a repeat customer who is prepared to pay for something akin to membership. This may well make sense for a journal - it is not very plausible for the individual book publisher as an individual may only infrequently want a book from a particular publisher. Some kind of sales consortium might be a solution here.

I am though dubious that scholars in the humanities and social sciences without research money will be very prepared to pay the quite high annual fee which this system would require. So while I believe it is an avenue for further exploration, I am not confident that this is the way to a full solution.

There is one related point that I do want to make. Some of the suggested solutions to the problems of academic publishing have eliminated the price mechanism altogether and suggested that academic publishing should be fully subsidized.

5.9. IPR AND COPYRIGHT ISSUES

Copyrights, together with patents, trademarks and industrial property rights, are part of a group of rights called "intellectual property rights." While the industrial property rights system is aimed at the development of the industrial economy, copyrights have as its aim the development of culture and the protection of copyright works such as music, paintings, novels, films and computer programs. The Copyright Law defines a copyright work as a "production in which thoughts or sentiments are expressed in a creative way and which falls within the literary, scientific, artistic or musical domain"

In Japan, copyrights differ from patents in that registration is not a requirement for acquiring the right; the right is born automatically at the time a work is created. Copyright, in a word, is a right that allows the copyright owner to permit (license) or prohibit the use of a copyright work to a person who wishes to use it. Therefore, aside from exceptions stipulated in the Copyright Law such as "reproduction for private use," it is necessary to obtain a license from the copyright owner when using copyright works.

Besides copyrights, the Copyright Law protects the rights of performers (singers and musicians), record producers (record labels and others), broadcasters and cable broadcasters, whose role is to disseminate copyright works to the general public, with rights called "neighboring rights." For instance, one music CD could include the rights of a lyricist and a composer (copyrights), as well as the rights of a record label and a singer or a musician (neighboring rights). So to upload music from a commercially available CD to an Internet website, it is necessary to obtain a license from the copyright owner (JASRAC if the work is administered by JASRAC) as well as from the neighboring rights owners.

Public recognition of copyrights and the extent of copyright protection afforded are said to be barometers of a country's cultural development. Respecting the important role that copyrights play in society, and to pay copyright owners a fair remuneration when using their works, will in turn lead to the creation of new copyright works and the development of culture.

5.9.1. Intellectual Property Rights

Intellectual property is an intangible creationof the human mind, usually expressed or translated into a tangible form that is assigned certain rights ofproperty. Every human being is endowed with certain but varying degree of intellect. Each individual isuniquely gifted. The word intellect originates from the root "intellectus" in Latin which means the power ofknowing as distinguished from the power to feel. Man has the capacity to acquire knowledge and increase his knowledge bank by gathering more and utilizing it as and when required throughout his life time. An intellectual makes his living by selling the product intellect, which is nothing but the brain child of his original idea, creative thought, which forms a special kind of property known as intellectual property. Aright as we know is legally protected interest and object of the right is the thing in which the owner has this interest. The object in intellectual property right is immaterial property.

IPR connotes the right to literary, artistic and scientific work; performances of performing artists; phonographs and broad-cast; inventions in all fields of human endeavor; scientific discoveries; industrial designs; trademarks; service marks and commercial names and designations, and all other products resulting from intellectual activity in the industrial, scientific, literary and artistic fields. It is a generic term covering patents; registered design; trademark; copyright; layout of integrated circuits, trade secrets; geographical indicators and anti-competitive practices in contractual licenses. Intellectual Property refers to creation of mind i.e. inventions, industrial designs for article, literary & artistic work, symbols etc. used in commerce

Intellectual property is divided into two categories: industrial property, which includes inventions(patents), trademarks, industrial designs, and geographic indications of source: and Copyright, which includes literary and artistic works such as novels, poems, plays, films and musical works etc. According to the TRIPS Agreement, the intellectual property has been classified into-Patents, Industrial Designs, Trade Marks, Copyright, Geographical Indications, Layout Designs of Integrated Circuits, and Protection of Undisclosed Information/Trade Secrets.

5.9.2. Copyright

In the early 2000s, many of the existing copyright laws were designed around printed books, magazines and newspapers. For example, copyright laws often set limits on how much of a book can be mechanically reproduced or copied. Electronic publishing raises new questions in relation to copyright, because if an e-book or e-journal is available online, millions of Internet users may be able to view a single electronic copy of the document, without any "copies" being made.

Emerging evidence suggests that e-publishing may be more collaborative than traditional paper-based publishing; e-publishing often involves more than one author, and the resulting works are more accessible, since they are published online. At the same time, the availability of published material online opens more doors for plagiarism, unauthorized use, or re-use of the material. Some publishers are trying to address these concerns. For example, in 2011, HarperCollins limited the number of times that one of its e-books could be lent in a public library. Other publishers, such as Penguin, are attempting to incorporate e-book elements into their regular paper publications.

The discussion in this session is divided into three areas: the basics of copyright and ownership of rights; licensing by authors to publishers and from publishers to users; and some of the economic and non-economic rewards to authors from scientific, technical, and medical (STM) publishing.

Before addressing the issues surrounding the grant of copyright from authors to publishers, it is important to review the "upstream" question of whether academic and research authors are initial copyright holders, or whether the institutions that employ them in fact hold the copyrights. The initial position matters for a variety of reasons, which need to be better understood. With regard to rights: What rights does copyright confer on authors (including the right to make available for free), and what rules govern the transfers of rights?

In terms of licensing, what rights can authors realistically give to or withhold from publishers? What are some alternative forms of managing rights, such as broad license to publishers while retaining copyright, and what are the pros and cons?

What are the major issues between the publishers and users of STM publications and of various models of access? Institutions generally gain access to electronic information via license. What kinds of access do these licenses offer? How could access be improved? What are the advantages and disadvantages of licensed access models compared with hard copy distribution? What role might the science funding agencies or other organizations play in resolving conflicts in relationships between authors and publishers, or publishers and users?

Finally, what are the current and potential economic and non-economic rewards to STM authors from publication, in both traditional and alternative venues? How else, apart from monetary compensation, can authors share in the value of their work? The Social Science Research Network (SSRN), an online publisher of abstracts and (when authors can provide it) full text for working papers or forthcoming published articles, is used as an example to explore these and other related issues in more detail.

5.9.3. Copyright Basics: Ownership and Rights

To begin this discussion, it is useful to examine three questions about copyright and scientific, technical, and medical publications. First, what rights does copyright establish, in what kinds of works? Second, who owns copyright in scholarly works? That is, does the academic author own the copyright, or does the university that employs her own the copyright? And third, assuming that the academic does own the copyright, what rights does she end up having to give up in order to get published?

5.9.4. Basic Rights Conferred by Copyright Law

With respect to copyright basics, first of all, copyright protects works of authorship, and that is a very broad notion. For example, it includes scientific works of all kinds, including computer software, whatever the medium of expression. Whether it is on paper, on film, or in ones and zeros, if it is a work of authorship, it is protected by the copyright law. It is important to understand, however, that while copyright protects the work, it does not protect the information as such within the work.

Copyright is one of the intellectual property rights which is automatically provided to the author or creator of original work, which gives them the exclusive right to reproduce and distribute the copyrighted work.

Copyright subsists in following original works:

- Literary works
- Dramatic works
- Musical works
- Artistic works
- Cinematographic works
- Sound recording

Copyrights protect two types of rights:

Economic rights : which allow the owner to derive financial reward from the use of their work by others.

Moral rights : which allow the owner of the original work to take certain actions to preserve and protect their work.

Term of Copyright

Copyright protection is granted to the author for a limited period, i.e. Life of Author + 60 Years.

5.9.5. Importance of Copyright

- It gives exclusive rights to the owner of original work to reproduce, duplicate, transcribe, and translate the work.
- The owner can prevent the misuse of their original work and can take legal action if infringement takes place.
- The owner has the sole right to get monetary benefits from their work.
- Encourages society for creativity as owners enjoy the

benefits and protection of their creative work.

5.9.6. Copyright Infringement

Owners develop new work and get copyright protection to ensure that they can get profit from their efforts. Owner has sole authority either to sell his work or to license it to the third party who can make use of his work but if someone duplicates or reproduces the work of copyright holder without the latter's permission, then this can lead to copyright infringement, in which owner can take legal action against the infringer.

Exception to Infringement under Sec.52 of The Copyright Act, 1957

- Private or personal use, including research
- Criticism or review, whether of that work or any other work
- The reporting of current events and current affairs, including the reporting of a lecture delivered in public.

5.9.7. Remedies for Infringement of Copyright

Civil remedy: According to Section 55 of The Copyright Act, 1957, where copyright in any work has been infringed upon, the owner of the copyright shall be entitled to all such remedies by way of injunction, damages, & accounts.

Criminal remedy : According to Section 63 of The Copyright Act, 1957, the copyright holder can take criminal proceedings against the infringer, in which there is a provision of at least six-month imprisonment, which may be extended to 3 years and with a fine of Rs. 50,000, which may extend to 2 lakhs.

Provided that if the defendant proves that at the date of the infringement he was not aware and had no reasonable ground for believing that copyright subsisted in the work, the plaintiff shall not be entitled to any remedy for the whole or part of the profits made by the defendant by the sale of the infringing copies as the court may in the circumstances deem reasonable.

Power of police to seize infringing copies : Any police officer, not below the rank of a sub-inspector, may, if he is satisfied that an offence under section 63 in respect of the infringement of copyright in any work has been committed, can seize copies without a warrant to produce before Magistrate.

5.9.8. The Rights protected by Copyright Law

Copyright law seeks to promote human creativity and confers several rights on the copyright owner. International agreements, among which the most important is the Berne Convention, 1886, seeks to standardize the rights available to copyright holders across different countries. The following rights will therefore be looked at as given in the Berne Convention to which most countries are signatories and whose provisions they have incorporated in their local laws as well.

Requirement of Originality : For any work to be eligible for copyright protection, the work needs to be original. The standard of originality is measured by the investment of labour, skill and judgement. In common law jurisdictions like United Kingdom and India, the standard of originality is low and even a low degree of investment in labour, skill and judgement will qualify for copyright protection. However, civil law jurisdictions like France and Germany demand certain minimum amount of creativity and author's intellectual expression.

Right of Reproduction : The most prominent is the right to reproduce, which implies making copies of the work in any form (Article 9). In the modern context copying a song on a CD would amount to reproduction. Sound and visual recordings are also considered as copying. Copying would amount to infringement unless it can be classified under one of the fair use defences. It is necessary to show that the person copying does not intend to make any commercial benefit out of it. In all other cases permission of the author is required.

Right to Distribute : An off-shoot right of reproduction is the right of distribution. The copyright owner may distribute his work in any manner he deems fit, he can even license it if he wishes or give it out on rent. The owner is at liberty to assign certain specific rights to somebody while retaining the rest; for example he may assign the right to make translations.

Right to make Derivative Works : Another important right that the owner has is to use the work in various ways, for instance while making adaptations (modifications in a work to suit some other requirements) (Article 12) or translations (converting from one language to another) (Article 11). Examples of adaptations would include making a movie based on a novel. Nobody else can make these derivative works without the owner's consent. Authors of literary and artistic works also have an additional right to make cinematographic adaptations and distribute the same (Article 14). In this context, related rights of the owner are also important, for instance, the right to integrity which protects the owner against distortion, mutilation or modification of his work in a way that it is harmful for his reputation.

Right to Publicly Perform : The copyright owner also has the right to publicly perform his works. Example, he may perform plays based on his work or perform at concerts, etc. Public does not have to be of a specific strength; even a large group of people would amount to performing before the public.

Right to Broadcast : A copyright owner also has the right to broadcast his work. Broadcasting would mean using of any means to make the work available to the public. In the modern context, this would extend to making the work accessible on the Internet. The terms and conditions of access will be decided by the copyright holder.

Right of Public Recitation : Authors of literary works are additionally conferred with the right to publicly recite their works

Right to Follow : A special right granted to authors is the right to obtain a percentage in the subsequent sales of his work and is called Droit de Suite or Right to Follow. The right is also available to artists on resale of their work.

Moral Rights : The moral rights required to be protected under the Berne Convention, Article 6bis are the "Right of Paternity" and the "Right of Integrity." These rights have been primarily adopted from the civil law jurisdictions which are more author centric, like France and Germany. They consider copyright to be more of a personal right of the author of the work, giving him credit for his intellectual effort and creativity. The Right of Paternity or Attribution gives the copyright owner a right to claim authorship of the work and the Right of Integrity gives the owner a right to prevent any distortion of the work which would be potentially harmful to the reputation and honour of the right holder. Under the Right of Paternity a copyright owner can claim due credit for any of his works. Thus, if a movie has been based on a book by an author, but he hasn't been given due credit in it, he can sue the makers to acknowledge his work. The Right to Integrity would protect a right holder if someone distorted, mutilated or modified his work in a way that it is harmful for his reputation and name. Economic rights can be licensed, but moral rights cannot. They remain with the author even if he has assigned or licensed his other rights. Therefore, altering or modifying any work may amount to infringement of an author's Right of Integrity unless written consent has been obtained for the same or it is reasonable under the circumstances to do so. Moral rights are protected more vigilantly in civil law countries. In fact, in USA, moral rights are only recognized for visual works and not for literary or musical works. Moral rights are considered more of a part of the law of defamation relating to libel and slander and do not get much importance otherwise.

Right to Enforce other Rights : The most important right available to copyright owners which makes all the other rights meaningful is the Right to Enforce Protected Rights (Article 15). Under this, the copyright holder can institute infringement proceedings against any violative work.

Private Copying: Private copying is an exception to the reproduction right in most countries as long as it does not jeopardize the interests of the right holders. Under the Berne Convention three step test, authors shall have the exclusive right to authorize reproduction of their works. However, member countries may by legislation permit the reproduction of the copyrighted works in certain specific cases, for example, private copying. It is in the interests of consumers to allow for private copying to a limited extent. The justification behind allowing private copying is that a single or limited act of copying made for the purpose of education or instruction should not be held as infringement. As long as there is no commercial motive behind copying and there is no harmful impact on the economic and non-economic rights of the copyright owner, there should be no restriction.

5.9.9. Collective Management Societies

Collective Management Societies as the name suggests are created with a view to collectively manage the rights of various copyright holders. These societies license the copyrighted works and collect royalties on behalf of the right owners. Royalty collection is the essential economic right of every copyright owner and it is not physically possible for him to discharge this function by himself. The problem is that there is generally only one such organization for each category of work, giving the society a near monopoly. Where there is monopoly, there is bound to be abuse and in order to protect the interests of both right holders and users, various steps maybe taken. One such method maybe trough Governmental regulation and supervision. Compliances maybe imposed on these societies threatening them with disbandment if they do not adhere to them. For example, the Indian Copyright Act,

1957 provides that if a copyright society is being managed in a manner detrimental to the interests of the right holders, its license can be cancelled. Secondly, an appellate body can be created to hear appeals against any conduct of the copyright society. This will provide copyright owners with a redressal mechanism in case the societies start charging arbitrary rates.

In any educational institute librarian plays a keyrole in many spheres, including copyright. The main role of librarian is to make available of library collections to students and faculty in support of teaching, learning, research and scholarship. Libraries are creatures of the historical and statutory balance in copyright law. Libraries lend materials based on the First Sale doctrine. Libraries share materials and preserve works under specific provisions for libraries in the Act. Libraries are often the only entities that provide access to the vast majority of copyrighted works that lose market vitality long before the expiration of the copyrights, and are often the only entities that preserve public domain materials. From the above perspective, it is clear and reasonable that the role of librarians is very important for the following reasons:

1. To enable users to access copyrighted and public domain works and to exercise their rights under the exceptions and limitations to creators rights in the law. The creation of new intellectual property building on the old is stimulated as a result of the existence of libraries. Libraries are places where public and the proprietary meet.
2. To work for library as social organizations address the balance in the law and are shaped by it. The institutional role of libraries, librarians and their associations necessitate paying close attention to that balance and promote users' rights as well as creators' rights. Libraries are a small but significant market for published works. The vast majority of copyrighted works in library collections were purchased or acquired through license

agreements. Often libraries pay more for copyrighted works than works of an individual. Hence, there is the need for library staff and users to know about copyright, their limitations and benefits, when making use of any of the materials on the library shelves, either in open or closed access in order to safeguard anti-piracy legislation. Libraries have an important role to play in caring for and providing access to other people's copyrighted work.

3. To recognize about copyrighted materials to the library users who are not aware of their dependence on balanced law and policy for access to information and for gaining knowledge.

4. To play a role as advocates for individual users of copyrighted materials. Librarians need to ensure that the rights and privileges of their customers are safeguarded i.e. they must assure the library users of uninhibited access to available collection in aid of research. Any user that is unsure if the material to be copied is protected by copyright needs to seek advice from the library staff.

5. To give the knowledge to the library users regarding "fair use legislation". This means that they can copy a very small amount of a work for educational purposes and not for commercial purposes. It may be possible to get permission to copy or use copyright material by contacting the copyright owner. Any copying now carried out for a commercial purpose requires prior permission from the copyright owner or payment of a copyright fee.

6. To give the orientation about rule of copyright infringement is the concept known as fair use. Under this principle, the law permits the use of portions of copyrighted works for such purposes as criticism, comment, teaching, and research, even without permission of the copyright owner.

7. There is a need for all the librarians in India to have copyright education in order to familiarize with the basic principles and concept of copyright laws in India. This will enable them to render their services without violating copyright laws. With adequate education in copyright, librarians will be able to know the risk involved in copying from copyright-protected material and operate within the laws. There is no doubt that libraries and Librarians in India have a lot of functions, very vital ones indeed, to play in the protection of author's rights. Firstly, they must provide the right guidance to their library users on how to make use of the library stock without infringing on the copyright of the authors of such works. The librarians can provide the following assistance to library users in order to properly enforce the copyright laws in the library. Research projects in the library should be made available to researchers for consultation only. Photocopying the entire work should not be allowed, and if there is the need to photocopy, the principle of fair use should be strictly adhered to. Also, the librarians should ensure that precise citation is done by any researcher for any piece of information collected from a given source in the Library.

5.10. SUMMARY

The purpose of copyright is to protect the rights of the owners of original work and provide economic benefits to them for their creativity and diligence. Although the registration of work is not necessary, but it is highly recommended to register as soon as one's idea is transforming into writings as it will be strong proof to be presented before the court in case of infringement. Therefore, it is strongly advised to avoid plagiarism.

5.11. REVIEW QUESTION

1. What is Economics of E-publishing?
2. What is copyright?
3. Define Collective Management Societies?

References

"Acrobat XI Pro FAQ". adobe.com. Adobe Systems. Archived from the original on 1 April 2015.

"Adobe Acrobat DC FAQ". helpx.adobe.com. Adobe Systems. Retrieved 20 August 2018.

"Adobe Acrobat family". 2008. Archived from the original on 19 January 2008. Retrieved 19 January 2008.

"Adobe Acrobat Professional software - Communicate and collaborate with the essential PDF solution, enhanced features for Central and East European and Middle Eastern users". Winsoft-international.com. Archived from the original on 31 August 2010.

"Adobe PDF Security Issues, Acrobat Vulnerabilities, PDF Cracks". Locklizard.

"Adobe Reader". 2008. Archived from the original on 18 January 2008. Retrieved 19 January 2008.

"Adobe Support Policies: Supported Product Versions". Adobe. 2016. Retrieved 20 October 2016.

"Security Bulletins and Advisories - Adobe Acrobat". adobe.com. Adobe Systems.

"Security Bulletins and Advisories". adobe.com. Adobe Systems. "The Definitive, Non-Technical Introduction to LaTeX, Professional Typesetting and Scientific Publishing". Math Vault. 2015-09-05. Retrieved 2019-07-18. *1994. SGML Web Page (http://www.sil.org/sgml/sgml.html)*

Abrams, S. L., Seaman, D.(2003). Towards a global digital format registry, Information Technology and Preservation and Conservation workshop, 2003, Berlin.

Amanda Presley (2010-01-28). "What Distinguishes Desktop Publishing From Word Processing?". Bright Hub. Retrieved 2019-05-02.

American Library Association. "ALA Survey of Public Library Services: A Summary Report." Chicago: ALA, Office for Research, 1987, typescript, p. 2.

Anthony Y. Fu, Wan Zhang, Xiaotie Deng, Liu Wenyin, 2006, Safeguard against Unicode attacks: generation and applications of UC-simlist, Proceedings of the 15th international conference on World Wide Web, Pages: 917 - 918 .

Anthony Y. Fu, Xiaotie Deng, Liu Wenyin, Greg Little, 2006, The methodology and an application to fight against Unicode attacks, ACM International Conference Proceeding Series, Vol. 149, Pages: 91 -101

Arora, (Jagdish). Building digital libraries: An overview. DESIDOC Bulletin of Information Technology. Vo1.21 (6); 2001; p3-24.

ASCII Table of just 0130-0255

Bear, Jacci Howard. "What's Involved in Desktop Publishing?". Lifewire. Retrieved 2019-05-02.

Bollen, J. and Luce, R. (2002). Evaluation of digital library impact and user communities by analysis of usage patterns. D-Lib Magazine, 8(6). Online, Available: http://www.dlib.org/dlib/june02/bollen/06bollen.html

Borgman, C. (2000). From Gutenberg to the global information infrastructure: access to information in the networked world. New York, ACM Press.

Borzo, Jeanette (14 June 1993). "Paperless: Tools resurrect hope for paperless office concept". InfoWorld. 15 (24). ISSN 0199-6649.

BOSC, H.; HARNAD, S. In a paperless world a new role for academic libraries: providing OA. *Learned Publishing*, v. 18, n. 2, p. 95-100, 2005.

Bradley, Neal. 1992. SGML concepts. *ASLIB proceedings 44, no. 7/8 (July/August): 271-274.*

Brinck, T., Gergle, D. and Wood, S. Usability for the Web: Designing Web Sites that Work. San Francisco, Morgan Kaufman, 2001.

Brown, A. (2006). Digital Preservation Technical Paper 2. The PRONOM Unique Identifier Scheme. DPTP-02, Issue2, p. 1-9. http://www.nationalarchives.gov.uk/aboutapps/pronom/pdf/pronom_unique_identifier_scheme.pdf

Bryan, Martin. 1988. *SGML: an authors' guide to the standard generalized markup language. Wokingham, Eng.: Addison-Wesley.*

Buckland, Michael. 1994. *From Catalog to Selecting Aid. From Catalog to Gateway, Briefings from the CFCC, no. 2, 1994 in ALCTS Newsletter 5, 1994.*

Burgin, Robert. "The User of Microcomputers Across Types of Libraries." Library Hi Tech News 34(Jan. 1987):1, 6-9.

Christensen, S. S. (2004) Archival data format requirements. Stats Bibliotek Report of the Royal Library, Denmark. *http://netarkivet.dk/publikationer/Archival_format_requirements2004.pdf*

CHUANG, J. C.; SIRBU, M. Networld delivery of information goods: optimal pricing or articles and subscriptions. In: KAHIN, B., VARIAN, H. R. (Ed.). *Internet publishing and beyond:* the economics of digital information and intellectual property. Cambridge, Mass: MIT Press, 2000. p.138-166.

CLARKE, R. Open source software and open content as models for eBusiness. In: INTERNATIONAL ECOMMERCE CONFERENCE, 17., 2004, Slovenia. *Electronic proceedings...* Disponívelem: <*http://www.anu.edu/people/Roger.Clarke/EC/Bled04.html*>. Acessoem: mar. 2006.

Clausen, L. R. (2004). Handling file formats. Stats Bibliotek. http://netarchive.dk/publikationer/FileFormats-2004.pdf

Cover, Robin. 1991. *Bibliography on SGML (Standard Generalized Markup Language) and related issues. Kingston, Ontario : Dept. of Computing and Information Science, Queen's University at Kingston.*

COX, J. Evolution or revolution in scholarly publishing. In: GORMAN, G. E; ROWLAND, F. (Ed.). *International yearbook of library and information management 2004/2005:* scholarly publishing in an Electronic Era. London: Facet Publishing, 2004. p. 54-74.

Craft (B) etal. Providing government information on the Internet: Experiment with THOMAS: In proceeding for geographically of digital libraries conference. DL 95, Austin TX. June 12-15, 1995, p19-25.

CROW, R. *The case for institutional repositories:* a SPARC position paper: the Scholarly Publishing & Academic Resources Coalition: release 1.0. 2002. Disponívelem: <*http://www.arl.org/ sparc/IR/ir.html*>. Acessoem: mar. 2006.

Davis, Stephen Paul. 1995. *Digital Image Collections: Cataloging Data Model & Network Access. (http://www.cc.columbia.edu/cu/libraries/inside/projects/diap/paper.html)*

Devika P. Madalli, July 2002, Unicode for multilingual representation in digital libraries from the Indian perspective, Proceedings of the 2nd ACM/IEEE-CS joint conference on Digital libraries

Digital preservation management: implementing short-term strategies for long term problems : online tutorial (2004) http://www.library.cornell.edu/preservation/tutorial/presentation/prese ntation-02.html

Eckerson, Wayne (26 July 1993). "Farallon gives Adobe Acrobat run for money". Network World. International Data Group. 10 (30): 86. ISSN 0887-7661.

F. Yergeau, 2003, UTF-8, a transformation format of ISO 10646 RFC Editor, United States.

FirdousMaqbool Mir, "Intellectual Property Rights Issues and Challenges of Academic Libraries in Digital Environment", International Journal Of Computer Engineering In Research Trends, 3(12):639-644-,December-2016. ©2016, IJCERT All Rights Reserved DOI:10.22362/ijcert/2016/v3/i12/xxxx Page | 640

Full Unicode format on Wikipedia

Gibson, W. 1993, Virtual light, Viking, London, 296 pp.

Guericio, M., Cappiello, C. (2004). File formats typology and registries for digital preservation, DELOS Report, 54 p. http://www.erpanet.org/events/2004/vienna/Vienna_Report.pdf

Hilbert, D. M and Redmiles, D. F. (2000). Extracting usability information from user interface events, ACM Computing Surveys. 32 (4), 384-421.

History of ASCII on ASCII-World

HTML Special Characters by the W3 consortium

http://en.wikipedia.org/wiki/Digital_library

http://hlwiki.slais.ubc.ca/index.php/Emerging_technology_librarians

http://toasterdog.com/files/basics_of_photoshop_full_guide.pdf

http://www.geocities.ws/namdevdeepak/upla_dl.htm

http://www.outsource2experts.com/PDFS/E-Publishing.pdf

https://www.adobe.com/devnet-docs/adobescan/ios/en/scan.html

https://www.g2.com/categories/desktop-publishing

HyLife (2002). The hybrid library toolkit. Interoperability. Available Http://hylife.unn.ac.uk/toolkit/Interoperability.html

Hypertext Markup Language - 2.0 (http://www.w3.org/hypertext/WWW/MarkUp/html-spec)

IANA character sets page

Internet Assigned Numbers Authority, "MIME Media Types", URL:http://www.iana.org/assignements/mediatypes/

Jarrin, Christopher (22 July 1996). "Reading what you sow". InfoWorld. 18 (30): 66. ISSN 0199-6649.

Jukka K. Korpela, 2006, Unicode Explained, 1st edition, Oreilly Publications.

Kannan, N. (2010). Importance of Intellectualproperty rights. International Journal ofIntellectual Property Rights, 1 (1), 1-5 RetrievedNovember

16th ,2016 from*http://iaeme.com/MasterAdmin/UploadFolder*IJIPR%20%20Importance%20of%20Intellectual%20Property%20Rights.pdf

Kent (Allen). Encyclopedia of Library and Information Science. Vol. 63; 1998, p259-77.

Kling, R. and Elliott, M. (1994). Digital library design for usability. Online. Available: http://www.csdl.tamu.edu/DL94/paper/kling.html (last accessed: 20/4/2004)

Kore, Sayali. C, Jadhav, Shital.T, Kadam, Amruta. S &Chavan, S. ushila. D. (2015).Introduction to Intellectual Property Right.Asian Journal of Pharmacy and Technology,5(4), 222-230.Retrieved November 16th, 2016 from*http://www.asianpharmaonline.org/pdf.php?j*=2231-5713&vol=5&issue=4&ab=ab176

Lancaster, F.W. 1995. The Evolution of Electronic Publishing. Library Trends, 43, 518-527.

List of Unicode characters on Wikipedia.

Marchiomini (G). Information Seeking in electronic environments. New York, Cambridge Press, 1995.

Marchionini, G. (1992). Interfaces for end-user information seeking, Journal of the American Society for Information Science, 43 (2), 1992, 156–63.

Marchionini, G. and Komlodi, A. (1998), 'Design of interfaces for information seeking'. In: Williams, M. E. (ed.), Annual review of information science and technology, Medford, NJ, Learned Information, 33, 1998, 89–130.

McKinney, Gayle, and Mosby, Ann Page. "Online in Academe: A Survey of Online Searching in U.S. Colleges and Universities." Online Review lO(Apri1 1986):115

Meyer P, 2005, "Planning a single source publishing application for business documents", Open Publish, Elkera Pty Limited,

Neethu Mohan, 2013. "Education at door steps of the poor', DC books education insider, vol. 2, issue 1, 78.

Panorama—SGML on the Web *(http://www.oclc.org:5047/oclc/research/panorama/)*

Prasad Pingali, JagadeeshJagarlamudi, VasudevaVarma, 2006, Indian language IR from multiple character encodings, Proceedings of the 15th international conference on World Wide Web, Pages: 801 - 809.

Rachchh, Manish.A.(2013). Module I- Basics ofIPR; Gujarat Technological University.Retrieved November 15th, 2016 fromhttp://www.gtu.ac.in/circulars/13Aug/Module1-BasicsofIPR_3rdAug2013.pdf

Richvalsky; Walkins. Designing and implementing a digital Library. ACM Crossroad student magazine. Jan 1998. http:// www.acm.org/ crossroads.rds5.2/ digital.html.

Roberts, P. 1999, 'Scholarly publishing, peer review and the Internet', First Monday, Volume 4, Issue 4. Accessed 20 December 2011, *http://www.firstmonday.dk/issues/issue4_4/proberts/index.html*

Rosati C, 2007, "Training Ground II: Single Sourcing in Action", IMPACT! The Newsletter of the Society for Technical Communication Marketing Communication SIG, vol. 12, no. 1, pp. 3 - 7.

Rothenberg, J. (1995). Ensuring the Longevity of Digital Documents. Scientific American, January 1995, p. 42-47.

Rubin, J. (1994), Handbook of Usability Testing: How to Plan, Design and Conduct Effective Tests, John Wiley & Sons, New York.

Ruiter, Maurice M. de (1988-04-29). Advances in Computer Graphics III. Springer Science & Business Media. ISBN 9783540187882.

Savage-Knepshield, P. A. and Belkin, N. J. (1999) Interaction in information retrieval: trends over time, Journal of the American Society for Information Science, 50 (12), 1999, 1067–82.

Sinha, Abhijeet&Bhardwaj, R.K. (2010).Digital Libraries and Intellectual PropertyRights. International Conference on DigitalLibraries. Retrieved November 15th , 2016from*https://rajkbhardwaj.files.wordpress.com/2014/*02/ art-9.pdf

Sinha, Abhijeet&Bhardwaj, R.K. (2010).Digital Libraries and Intellectual PropertyRights. International Conference on DigitalLibraries. Retrieved November 15th, 2016from*https://rajkbhardwaj.files.wordpress.com/2014/*02/ art-9.pdf

Stephanie Strassel, Mike Maxwell, Christopher Cieri, June 2003, Linguistic resource creation for research and technology development: A recent experiment, ACM Transactions on Asian Language Information 155 Processing (TALIP), v.2 n.2, p.101-117.

Tetsuo Sakaguchi, Akira Maeda, Takehisa Fujita, Shigeo Sugimoto, Koichi Tabata, 1996, A browsing tool of multi-lingual documents for users without multi-lingual fonts, Proceedings of the first ACM international conference on Digital libraries, Pages: 63-71.

Thakur. D.S. 2005, "Approaches to Knowledge Management in higher education".

The Representation and Rendering Project, University of Leeds: "Survey and assessment of sources of information on file formats and software documentation, Final Report", 2003, URL:http: / / www.jisc.ac.uk/ uploaded_documents / FileFormatsreport.p df

UNESCO 1996. The Legal Deposit of Electronic Publications: Working Group of the Conference of Directors of National Libraries. Paris: UNESCO.

Van House, N., Butler, M.H., Ogle, V. and Schiff, L. (1996). User-centred iterative design for digital libraries: the Cypress experience. D-Lib Magazine. Online. Available: http://www.dlib.org/dlib/february96/02vanhouse.html

White, M. (2002). Information architecture and usability, EContent. 2002. 25 (4), 46-47.

Wiederhold (G). Mediation in the architecture of future information systems. IEEE Computer. Vol. 38-49; March 1992.

Wilson, R. and Landoni, M. (2003). Evaluating the Usability of Portable Electronic Books. Proceedings of the 2003 ACM Symposium on Applied Computing (SAC), March 9-12, 2003, Melbourne, FL, USA. ACM: pp. 564-568